T0305925

Strategic University Management

Universities are being buffeted by multiple disruptive trends, including increased competition for both funding and students, as well as from new institutions that are nimbler and more responsive to the external environment. To survive this reality, university leaders must engage in effective strategic planning that cascades from the president's office to individual faculty and staff. Outcomes of an effective institutional strategy are the alignment of resource allocation with strategic goals, and the facilitation of clear and transparent decision-making for new programme development, research capacity growth, and infrastructure investment.

With increasing expectations for university leaders to engage in strategic planning, *Strategic University Management: Future-Proofing Your Institution* provides a practical framework for managing the process and delivering results. This book illustrates that the inherent weaving of strategic planning and organisational culture through engaged consultation facilitates a culture of responsiveness, rather than complacency.

Providing an in-depth overview of the value that strategy can create in universities provides a framework for initiating, implementing, and assessing strategic planning in a university setting that will make it valuable to researchers, academics, university leaders, and students in the fields of strategic planning, organisational studies, leadership, and higher education management.

Loren Falkenberg was Senior Associate Dean of Graduate and Professional Programs in the Haskayne School of Business at the University of Calgary, Canada.

M. Elizabeth Cannon is President Emerita at the University of Calgary, Canada.

Routledge Focus on Business and Management

The fields of business and management have grown exponentially as areas of research and education. This growth presents challenges for readers trying to keep up with the latest important insights. Routledge Focus on Business and Management presents small books on big topics and how they intersect with the world of business research.

Individually, each title in the series provides coverage of a key academic topic, whilst collectively, the series forms a comprehensive collection across the business disciplines.

The Customer Experience Model
Adyl Aliekperov

Organizational Justice and Organizational Change
Managing By Love
Dominique A. David

Cultural Proximity and Organization
Managing Diversity and Innovation
Federica Ceci and Francesca Masciarelli

Entrepreneurial Urban Regeneration
Business Improvement Districts as a Form of Organizational Innovation
Rezart Prifti and Fatma Jaupi

Strategic University Management
Future-Proofing Your Institution
Loren Falkenberg and M. Elizabeth Cannon

For more information about this series, please visit: www.routledge.com/ Routledge-Focus-on-Business-and-Management/book-series/FBM

Strategic University Management
Future-Proofing Your Institution

**Loren Falkenberg and
M. Elizabeth Cannon**

Routledge
Taylor & Francis Group

NEW YORK AND LONDON

First published 2021
by Routledge
52 Vanderbilt Avenue, New York, NY 10017

and by Routledge
2 Park Square, Milton Park, Abingdon, Oxon, OX14 4RN

Routledge is an imprint of the Taylor & Francis Group, an informa business

Library of Congress Cataloging-in-Publication Data
Names: Falkenberg, Loren E., author. | Cannon, M. Elizabeth (Margaret
    Elizabeth), 1962-
Title: Strategic university management : future proofing your institution /
    Loren Falkenberg and M. Elizabeth Cannon.
Description: New York, NY : Routledge, 2021. | Series: Routledge focus
    on business and management | Includes bibliographical references and
    index.
Identifiers: LCCN 2020031238 (print) | LCCN 2020031239 (ebook) |
    ISBN 9780367522636 (hardback) | ISBN 9781003057222 (ebook)
Subjects: LCSH: Universities and colleges—Administration. | Universities
    and colleges—Planning. | Universities and colleges—Business
    management. | Strategic planning. | Education and globalization.
Classification: LCC LB2341 .F328 2021 (print) | LCC LB2341 (ebook) |
    DDC 378.1/01—dc23
LC record available at https://lccn.loc.gov/2020031238
LC ebook record available at https://lccn.loc.gov/2020031239

ISBN: 978-0-367-52263-6 (hbk)
ISBN: 978-1-003-05722-2 (ebk)

Typeset in Times New Roman
by Apex CoVantage, LLC

Contents

Tables

Figures

Acknowledgments

The authors would like to thank their colleagues, past and present, who contributed to the development and implementation of the Eyes High strategy at the University of Calgary which provided the motivation to write this book. This strategy led to the university significantly elevating its impact and reputation, which inspired us to capture the experience and learnings for broader dissemination to the higher education community. The success of Eyes High was a result of the collective commitment of institutional leaders, board members, faculty, staff, students, alumni, and community leaders. Their efforts and continued support are acknowledged and appreciated. The authors would like to particularly thank Bruce Evelyn for his advice and perspectives into higher education strategic planning, and Jim Dewald and Pari Johnston for their thoughtful feedback.

Loren Falkenberg & Elizabeth Cannon

Preface

Higher education institutions are having to adapt to an increasingly competitive global environment. While in some emerging economies new institutions are being launched or expanded to grow capacity and meet demand, in mature economies there are mergers or closures due to overcapacity or an inability to be nimble and responsive to the external environment. COVID-19 has accelerated the impact of disruptive technologies in terms of where and how educational programmes are delivered, and has increased competition for students. Governments are expecting higher levels of accountability for publicly funded universities, global ranking systems are influencing reputations and students' choices, and financial support is shifting from public to alternative funding sources. To survive this new reality, higher education leaders must engage in strategic planning that cascades from the president's office to individual faculty and staff and beyond the walls of the institution, so it can be prepared for an uncertain future.

Higher education leaders, in comparison to their business counterparts, are often relatively unprepared to lead and engage in strategic planning. Business strategy is a separate and active field of research in business schools, with 17 specialised peer-reviewed journals dedicated to the topic, in addition to numerous professional degree programmes which teach strategy as a topic. Although there are over 28,000 universities globally, there are no dedicated research journals on strategy theory or practice in higher education. Academic institutions have a very different operating context from that of business organisations; they have relatively flat structures with complex governance systems, largely dependent on governments or private donors for funding, with relatively independent faculty—their key resource—and significant fixed assets. The lack of scholarly work dedicated to higher education strategic planning has created a substantial knowledge gap for academics moving into significant leadership positions.

During their career progression to the top of their organisations, most business leaders participate in strategy training and planning sessions, and are involved in the implementation of strategic plans. In contrast, many leaders in higher education have minimal opportunities to develop their knowledge or skills in strategic planning, let alone to lead the development and implementation of a strategic plan for a large faculty or unit. They do not usually hold administration or business degrees, nor have they attended extensive executive education training in higher education. The result is that knowledge of, and confidence in, strategic planning is not a deep skill set in this group.

This book fills this knowledge gap for higher education leaders. The authors led two distinct strategic planning processes at the University of Calgary in 2010–11 and 2016–17, and based upon this experience developed a framework for strategic planning and implementation in academic institutions. The complementary relationship of the authors (a former university president and a business professor) provides a unique lens for strategic planning in higher education. The theories integrated into this framework, adapted from research published in business journals and augmented by available literature in higher education, increase the relevance of the book to the broader academic environment and its leaders. More importantly, these strategies were successfully applied twice at the University of Calgary.

One of the differences between higher education and business is the diffuse, diverse, and independent nature of academic faculty. Although some argue the independence of faculty members and the diversity of their activities reduce the impact of institutional strategic planning, the authors believe these factors increase the need to prepare academic institutions for an uncertain future. Academic freedom, tenure, and a lack of a unifying metric (e.g., profitability) require different approaches to strategic planning than occur in most businesses. Although these factors can be obstacles to universities effectively responding to disruptive forces, they can also provide the foundation for creating and disseminating knowledge that is highly valued by society. An effective institutional strategy coordinates and guides independent faculty activities towards a sustainable future. In response to challenges in the higher education environment, this book answers three questions: How can an institutional strategy ensure that an academic institution has a unifying vision to drive its future in an uncertain environment? What are the key components and processes needed to create future-oriented institutional strategies? And, how can a higher education leader create alignment between strategy, goals, decisions, and culture so the institution is future-proofed?

Chapter 1 outlines the unique features of an academic environment in contrast to business organisations, and the need to build a strategy that is responsive to this environment and the future. Chapter 2 focuses on the role of a president in initiating and overseeing the strategic planning process, particularly in identifying the level of change required. The need to weave strategy and institutional culture together as the foundation for informed engagement, as well as the communication of the consultation findings to stakeholders, are discussed in Chapter 3. Chapter 4 describes the process to identify gaps and develop a unified strategy which "simplifies complexity" to create a sustainable future. The last two chapters focus on establishing a line-of-sight to ensure leaders understand their role in achieving the strategic goals and building an effective institutional culture. The appendix describes the application of the strategic planning process, and its resulting impacts, through a case study at the University of Calgary.

The overall outcomes of an effective institutional strategy are the alignment of resource allocation with strategic goals, and the facilitation of clear and transparent decision-making in teaching, research, and community engagement. These outcomes on their own are sufficient justification for the costs of developing strategic plans; however there are others that contribute more value. Although some faculty may not agree with the strategic priorities, such as the allocation of resources to one particular area rather than another, they are more likely to accept them rather than actively resist if they understand the logic and intended outcomes. If the strategic planning processes are based on informed consultation, the planning process can nurture an effective institutional culture which is responsive and resilient. In particular, a well-executed strategy attracts new investment, increases recognition, and improves reputation, which benefits all stakeholders. Thus, the saying "a rising tide lifts all boats" applies when a strategic plan has a broad positive impact on the institution. The key for adoption of a strategy is not necessarily agreement with the priorities; rather it is a combination of factors: the visibility of the strategic priorities, the logic behind the priorities, consistent decisions, and the evaluation of progress towards the goals.

Given the increasing need for universities to prepare for an uncertain future through strategic planning, this book provides a practical framework for managing the process. This framework is an integration and adaptation of a broad range of academic disciplines, including strategic management, stakeholder consultation, qualitative research methodologies, and project management. Components of the strategic planning and implementation processes at the University of Calgary are used to develop a practical roadmap for academic leaders and their planning teams. A key message of the book is the inherent weaving of strategy and institutional culture through informed consultation and consistent communication.

The framework simplifies strategic planning into clear, actionable phases from the first responsibilities of the leader to set the stage, to development, implementation, and, finally, assessment of the strategy's impact. The book is structured so leaders can "slice and dice" the various phases into a process that is nuanced to the needs of their institution. Adapting the framework to the context of a given institution leads to savings in resources, including, perhaps most importantly, time.

The governance structure of higher education institutions brings together individuals with differing perspectives and experiences of how to manage and coordinate the activities of a university. This can lead to either conflict or a positive impact on the institution's future. After reading the book, university board members should have a better understanding of the organised chaos of academic institutions and how internal dynamics limit a more authoritarian response to external disruptions. They will appreciate the importance of broad stakeholder engagement in strategy development to build alignment and support of diverse constituents. They will see an institutional strategy as an unwritten contract between the board and the president, which can drive transformation and change while managing expectations by stakeholders.

Most higher education presidents have an implicit knowledge of the tensions within the academy; however, they do not have frameworks on how to strategically manage them in order to build cohesive responses to the external environment. Chapters 1 to 4 provide a framework to raise this implicit knowledge to an explicit and intentional level so that strategic planning becomes a unifying, rather than divisive, process. These chapters also review the role of institutional culture in shaping the strategy and its success by embracing change while building resilience and responsiveness. Chapters 5 and 6 provide a roadmap to execute the institutional strategy through operational planning, and ongoing communication and enhancement of an effective institutional culture.

After reading the book, members of the president's executive team, particularly those who have not been faculty members in their careers, will have a better understanding of how to manage the organised chaos of academic institutions, and the need for transparent goals which all stakeholders— particularly faculty and staff—have developed in collaboration (Chapters 1 and 2). They will also understand the need for strategy to guide their operational planning and budget decisions (Chapters 5 and 6). Institutional planners will have a better understanding of the phases involved in strategic planning and their role in supporting the process through information gathering, data analysis, and priority-setting (Chapters 2 to 4). They will also appreciate the linkages between strategy and operations, and the role of business plans to course correct in a changing external environment (Chapters 5 and 6).

Deans and other leaders of academic units will have a more explicit understanding of the tensions they experience in managing their faculties, particularly between the teaching and research pillars (Chapter 1). They will also have a better understanding of the value created by an institutional strategy, and the need to align their faculty's strategy with the broader needs of the institution (Chapter 2). They can adapt the strategic planning processes outlined in Chapters 2 to 4 to their particular unit, and then link their faculty's strategy to operational planning and execution (Chapters 5 and 6).

Finally, this book is also relevant to strategy researchers who will have an increased understanding of the issues associated with strategic planning in higher education, and where future research should focus. Given the nascent field of strategy research in higher education and the rapidly growing disruptive forces influencing universities' contributions to society , it is important to better understand how universities can create strategies to ensure they remain valued institutions.

1   Institutional Dynamics and the Role of Strategy

The once stable environment of higher education is shifting into a turbulent and increasingly competitive marketplace, where universities can no longer just graduate students or produce ground-breaking research; they now must also be "future ready" (EY, 2018). Two contrasting trends reflect the disruptions occurring in higher education. One is the growth in new universities and the "massification" of higher education in jurisdictions such as Asia (UNESCO Institute for Statistics, 2014), while in more developed economies there are cases of declining enrolments (NSC Research Center, 2019), and even mergers and closures of institutions. Uncertainty as to the future status of universities is growing with new technologies disrupting programme delivery, governments requiring more formal planning and accountability, university rankings influencing reputations, and a shift from public to alternative funding sources. This new reality has increased the need for university leaders to engage the whole campus in strategic planning and, equally as important, ensure that the strategy cascades from the president's office to faculty, staff, and external stakeholders. The COVID pandemic has only increased the rate at which these disruptive forces are impacting university operations. Yet, more often than not, universities spend significant resources on strategic planning and then do nothing until the next round of planning (Pritchard, 2018; Robertson & Olds, 2018).

While the external environment has become turbulent, the internal dynamics of universities have been slow to change. Faculty members, and some staff, operate in the traditional silos of their departments or disciplines, focusing on remaining relevant with their research colleagues. They have little interest in campus-wide events and activities in other faculties, and minimal interest in the dynamics of the higher education sector. As long as individuals have the resources they need, there is little thought about institutional efficiency or overall effectiveness (Porck et al., 2018).

The traditional culture of faculty silos has led to a growing and significant gap between the external and internal realities of universities. This chapter explores this gap and the need for strategies that bridge it, without destroying the centuries-long mandate of universities: to push the boundaries of curiosity and thought leadership.

Internal Dynamics and External Disruptions

Universities are unique institutions. Unlike a corporation with specific products or services to sell, they are more akin to a city, encompassing a broad range of activities, and "have almost no internal agreement about what they are" (Usher, 2019a). Researchers have described universities as "organised chaos," arising from the independence of faculty who are protected by academic freedom and tenure (Cohen & March, 1974; Leih & Teece, 2016). Others argue labelling the chaos "organised" is generous, given that academic leaders have significantly less control over faculty activities than corporate executives have over their employees' work. Strategy development is influenced by the internal dynamics contributing to the chaos, as well as external disruptions that compound the tensions inside universities.

A critical factor influencing the development and execution of strategy is the external orientation of many faculty members. Research-oriented faculty are socialised, from the day they enter graduate school, to build an academic reputation through the external activities of publishing and conference presentations. As well, many are dependent on external research funding. Universities reinforce this outward focus by requiring external referees for tenure and promotion, and establishing merit-based external metrics (e.g., citations, recognition of critics). Although many argue this approach leads to independent thought in research and teaching materials, an external focus can sideline researchers' commitment to their university, and hence support for a unifying institutional strategy (Pai, Yeh & Huang, 2012). And, part-time or sessional instructors often teach at more than one institution and focus on building a broad teaching portfolio with little interest in the strategic needs of a particular institution.

Most universities have mandates in three areas—or pillars—which are teaching and learning ("teaching"), research and scholarship ("research"), and community service (sometimes referred to as "community engagement"). An internal dynamic influencing an institution's strategic goals is the systemic tension between the teaching and research pillars. Studies show that teaching and research are viewed as independent activities competing for financial resources, space, and qualified faculty (Hattie & Marsh, 1996), even when faculty believe they should be good at both (Brew, 2003; Webster, 1985). Adding to this tension are the global ranking systems which focus on research outcomes, with little consideration given to teaching effectiveness. This tension leads to reinforcement of existing beliefs as to which set of activities should be prioritised rather than flexibility in shifting priorities.

Within the research pillar, the perceived value of different types of research is continually questioned (Checkoway, 2001). Scholars in the sciences and social sciences/humanities are socialised to freely experiment with new ideas independent of immediate relevance (Grey, 2001; Heracleous, 2011); while those in professional schools value pragmatic or more immediately applicable knowledge (Grey, 2001; Heracleous, 2011; Kondrat, 1992; Nicolai, 2004; Simon, 1976; Tranfield & Starkey, 1998; Van de Ven & Johnson, 2006). Currently, many social science faculty are resisting the growing expectation that universities should be key contributors to innovation and the commercialisation of knowledge (Mowery & Sampat, 2005); they counterargue that many of the advances known today came from exploratory research on ideas that did not originally have a visible pragmatic outcome.

Within the teaching pillar, there is systemic tension between the traditional liberal arts education, which develops disciplinary knowledge and skills based on a student's passion, and the professional schools, which build the knowledge and skills relevant to a specific career (Grey, 2001; Heracleous, 2011; Kondrat, 1992; Nicolai, 2004; Tranfield & Starkey, 1998; Van de Ven & Johnson, 2006). Both types of education are important to society. A liberal arts education leads to critical thinking and well-developed communication skills, as well as the ability to apply interdisciplinary knowledge when analysing problems (Zakaria, 2015). Many undergraduates are able to apply their interdisciplinary knowledge to complex societal problems. In contrast, a technical education is responsive to the economy's need for skilled labour and applied research. The value of a narrower technical education is reflected in the success of universities such as the Massachusetts Institute of Technology and the Technical University of Munich (Altmann & Ebersberger, 2012; Youtie & Shapira, 2008). Again, these tensions often reinforce existing faculty silos rather than adopting a broader university perspective.

The higher education environment is experiencing increased turbulence from multiple disruptive technologies, particularly in the teaching pillar (De Boer et al., 2002). The impending disruption of technology platforms which effectively deliver course material into students' own digital spaces is increasing the possibilities of learning from internationally recognised professors located anywhere in the world (Altbach, Reisberg & Rumbley, 2009), with COVID-19 rapidly accelerating the impact of these platforms. In parallel, non-academic organisations offering certificates through bundling skills via online learning are flourishing (Dusst & Winthrop, 2019). These organisations are nimble and responsive to student needs as they are not hampered by the bureaucracy systemic in established universities.

The hyper-expansion of expectations for universities, including democratisation, human rights, scientisation, and development planning (Schofer & Meyer, 2005) have created ambiguity as to their mandate (Youtie & Shapira, 2008). As noted by Morphew, Fumasoli and Stensaker (2016), "a recurring theme of higher education research is the blurring boundaries of functions, objectives, and scope of universities, due to the increased emphasis on relevance, service to society, and changes in the modes of knowledge production." Part of this hyper-expansion is the expectation that universities will work with communities in finding solutions to local and global social problems (Etzkowitz et al., 2000; Etzkowitz, 2003; Laredo, 2007; Usher, 2018a). They are expected to partner with business and not-for-profit organisations to fund innovation and social enterprises (Slaughter & Leslie, 1997). This emerging threefold interaction among universities, government, and civil society has been labelled a triple helix and demonstrates the importance for academic institutions to consider other actors in the system when considering their own futures (Etzkowitz & Leydesdorff, 1999).

The global and national ranking of universities has created a system over which academic leaders have little control but must still monitor because where an institution places in the better-known ranking surveys has notable reputational and operational consequences (Tamburri, 2013). Although the ranking of universities has been around for decades, prior to 2003 it was dependent on self-completed surveys, which were difficult to collect and had minimal impact. In 2003 a Chinese scholar began gathering bibliometric measures of publications, citations, and major awards of universities around the globe (Usher, 2018b). This led to a rapid adoption of the methodology and an increase in the number of ranking organisations. The irony is that universities are unlikely to move more than one or two places in a given decade, and the top ten institutions will generally remain in the top ten (Usher, 2018c). However, administrators cannot ignore the rankings and must guide their institutions towards achieving metrics that keep them from losing ground in their placement.

Reputation is a criteria included in most of the rankings; and this is a strategic outcome that most universities can control. Reputation is built by providing valued and unique programmes and, when established, has greater influence with key stakeholders than rankings. Most universities should be more concerned about their reputation with their primary stakeholders than their exact placement in the rankings. However, without a strategy that is shared across the institution, it is difficult to coordinate the resources and activities needed to build or enhance a positive reputation.

In summary, the academy must now compete *for students,* operate *with reduced funding,* adjust *to changing technologies and demographics,* and respond *to the growing complexity of societal problems.* Each university must align and differentiate its programmes to the expectations of its stakeholders rather than adopt a universal approach (Strike, Hanlon & Foster, 2018). They must find the appropriate balance between building programmes that create value for identified stakeholders and creating knowledge for the sake of new knowledge (Shin, 2017; Yorke, 2004).

Strategy as a Bridge

Successful business leaders are constantly aware of their external environments and develop strategies to satisfy market demands. The importance of strategic planning in a market-based economy is reflected in the extensive research and popular literature on business strategies. Although universities and businesses have different mandates and operating contexts, this literature is still relevant to higher education. Universities are focused on producing a public good rather than maximizing profit; they have more time to respond to disruptions, and they apply a different set of metrics to measure success (Strike, 2018). However, as competition grows in the higher education sector there is an increasing need to adapt the findings in business strategy research to the new realities of higher education.

An effective institutional strategy explicitly states where the university should be in the future (usually five years), identifies the gaps that need to be bridged to achieve the goals, and guides decision-making throughout the organisation (Pritchard, 2018; Rumelt, 2012). It is different from the university's mission (Collis & Rukstad, 2008). The mission identifies the contribution a university intends to make, through its education, and knowledge creation and dissemination. Universities share very similar missions; however, each university operates in a unique context, with differing combinations of strengths, weaknesses, and potential to respond to opportunities and reduce risks. A strategy is based on these unique combinations. It sets the priorities for difficult decisions on resource allocation and guides decisions as to what programmes the university will or will not support (Porter, 1996). It involves setting goals and identifying metrics to measure progress towards the goals.

An institutional strategy is not about operational effectiveness. Strategy involves developing new activities or performing similar activities in different ways. Operational effectiveness involves performing a specific activity in an efficient way (Porter, 1996). A future-proofed university makes strategic choices on the activities or combination of activities that need to be in place five to 10 years into the future, while ensuring operational effectiveness is monitored and enhanced.

In comparison to business organisations, universities are not nimble, as they cannot change direction over a short time frame. Universities are more like an urban community than a business organisation, with housing, recreational facilities, parking, public events, and academic faculties all operating as independent units. Within these units are expensive physical assets such as specialised laboratories, classrooms, and libraries which require constant maintenance. As well, the academic units have tenured faculty, whose careers with the institution can span more than 20 or 30 years. Knowledge that their careers continue long after a particular leader has come and gone builds inertia and resistance to change.

University leaders cannot easily sell or eliminate the institution's physical assets or reduce tenured faculty in order to change direction or respond to disruptive trends. Each of these independent units recognises the impact of external forces operating on their unit, but not the combined external forces on the institution as a whole. Ironically, publicly funded institutions are dependent on the short-term orientations of governments, with little flexibility to respond to new initiatives. A logical conclusion would be that a straightforward, or simple, strategy cannot balance the complexities associated with managing a university. Conversely, it is indeed a simple strategy that is needed to coordinate and align these disparate groups, and reduce the existing isolated decision-making that leads to narrow, short-term responses to external disruptions.

The work of three McKinsey consultants in the late 1990s provides a simple visualisation of the role of strategy in connecting a university's current operations with emerging and potential areas of growth (Baghai, Coley & White, 2000). The three horizons on Figure 1.1 illustrate how a strategy

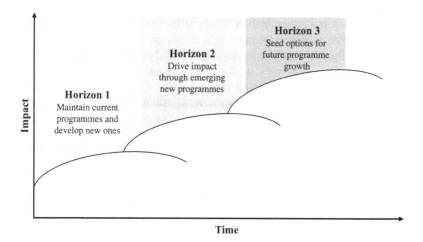

Figure 1.1 Strategic Planning Over Three Time Horizons

Source: (adapted from Baghai, Coley & White, 2000)

reinforces current operations while preparing for anticipated future disruptions. Strategic planning processes should review the effectiveness of programmes under Horizon 1, while identifying the opportunities and risks under Horizons 2 and 3, with the resulting strategy guiding the institution towards those Horizons.

Horizon 1 covers the university's current programmes, which include core programmes or the basic undergraduate and graduate programmes, common to most universities. These are often described as the building blocks of disciplinary fields of knowledge (e.g., chemistry, psychology, law). Although the assumption is that these programmes are critical to a university's mission, they require regular reviews, as not every university should provide a complete suite of academic disciplines. Clark (1998:p.6) noted that "academic departments based on disciplinary fields of knowledge will go on being important: their disciplinary competence is essential, too valuable to throw away, and they have much power with which to protect their own domains. But the departments alone cannot do all the things that universities now need to do."

Also included under Horizon 1 are programmes specifically aligned to the institution's environment and unique combination of stakeholders, and not offered by other universities (Asheim & Coenen, 2005; Liu & White, 2001; Porter, 1996). Often they are an extension of conventional disciplinary fields, with specific expertise and unique research infrastructure developed to meet community or primary constituent needs (e.g., major employment sectors or industries). The need for, and content of, these programmes evolves over time. Thus, a first step in strategic planning is a review of both types of current programmes to assess which should be continued as the foundation of the institution's activities, and receive sufficient and appropriate resources to be offered in the most cost efficient or effective manner (Porter, 1996), and which should be reduced, modified, or abandoned over the next five years.

The programmes listed under Horizon 2 are those that will be needed in five years (although these time lines are being compressed with the increased need to be more responsive). They include the programmes in Horizon 1 that will still be relevant, and new programmes that should be ready in five years' time. New programmes should increase the impact of the university over the next five years. The need to work through these two time horizons is critical as it can take more than five years for universities to develop the capacity to offer new programmes. If new research infrastructure, methods of curriculum delivery, and expertise are needed in Horizon 2, university leaders have to initiate steps in Horizon 1 to ensure they are in place, or they risk losing growth opportunities or having to invest in additional resources to play catch-up.

Under Horizon 3 are programmes that may be needed in 10-years' time. Given the uncertainty associated with a 10-year timeframe, leaders should be ensuring there is sufficient flexibility in the system to respond to these opportunities if they actually become viable. Given the fixed nature of university resources—both physical assets and tenured faculty—it may take up to 10 years to respond to emerging trends, so monitoring for potential disruptions in Horizon 3 is critical. Basing an institutional strategy on these three horizons ensures relevancy and sustainability of a university's programmes.

The adoption of a five-year window for a strategic plan is driven by a need to be future-oriented while ensuring urgency is created in the implementation of the strategy and the impact on the institution. Although the strategy will a focus on five-year goals, it should be looking forward to a longer time horizon. Five-year strategic plans are assumed throughout the remainder of the book.

Outcomes of Effective Institutional Strategies

The "currency" in higher education is reputation—it is how universities distinguish themselves and the programmes they offer and attract high quality students, faculty, and additional financial support. A well-developed and implemented strategy is the most effective approach to building a university's local, national, and international reputation (Leih & Teece, 2016). University reputations are established through a complex combination of activities and expertise; without a strategy these activities may become chaotic as opposed to intentional. Building a reputation occurs over decades, and requires offering programmes, both conventional and specialised, that are aligned with community expectations. For instance, publicly funded universities must provide equal and affordable access to higher education, and have a reputation for educating and placing their graduates in the job market (Neave, 1989). Highly ranked universities have a reputation for preparing political and business leaders, which attracts funding from alumni in leadership positions.

An effective institutional strategy reduces political conflicts (Nelson & Winter, 1982) by simplifying decision-making through visible priorities and attention on a limited number of strategic choices (Ocasio & Joseph, 2018). If a university strategy has been developed through campus-wide engagement, it is easier for university leaders to justify these priorities because of the transparency followed in developing them (Cohen & March, 1974). A campus is comprised of competing viewpoints across multiple stakeholders, including board members, community leaders, students, faculty members, and funders, and it is easier to manage tensions when all parties believe they were heard.

A strategic planning process builds the foundation for an effective institutional culture which, in turn, creates responsiveness to external disruptions. The phrase "culture eats strategy for breakfast" (Teasdale, 2002) reflects the need for leaders to attend to both strategy and culture. Every year hundreds of books are published on the value of a unifying culture in business organisations, with limited attention given to effective cultures in higher education. University cultures are based on academic freedom, where independent scholarship and thinking is valued. It is important, however, to differentiate between academic culture, which exists across the higher education sector broadly, and institutional culture, which reflects the norms, expectations, and behaviours within a specific institution. University leaders need to continually communicate respect for academic freedom while reinforcing the need for responsiveness to internal or external challenges through a transparent institutional culture. Although the idea of a "unifying" culture may be perceived as limiting creativity by faculty members, a focus on the understanding and development of an effective institutional culture has been shown to be critical to driving change and performance in the academic sector (Kezar & Eckel, 2002; Taye, Sang & Muthanna, 2019).

Strategy cannot change the multiple sub-cultures within the three pillars and various units of a university; it can, however, unify the campus by reinforcing an overriding institutional culture of responsiveness (Porck et al., 2018). The traditional culture of silos occurs because administration and faculties operate independently, limiting unified responses to the external environment. These culture silos reward faculty members for responding to disruptions or changes in their specific discipline, while ignoring campus-wide issues. An effective strategy reduces the impact of thinking in silos and harnesses the collective ambition and action of the entire campus.

An effective and responsive culture is based on respect for differing points of view and the inclusiveness of a broad range of stakeholders. A strategic planning process must respect the diversity of an institution's constituents and consider the disparate views these constituents hold. Not everyone will agree on the final strategy, but when the planning process is built on respect and inclusion there is a broader acceptance of the difficult choices associated with a strategy and its implementation. If the strategic planning process does not signal the need to bridge the internal dynamics of a university with its external environment, faculty silos are reinforced and the strategy is difficult to implement, leading to an erosion of the institution's reputation. Although difficult decisions are required in the development and implementation of a strategic plan, openness and transparency about the necessary trade-offs reinforce an effective institutional culture (Tierney, 1988).

Failed Institutional Strategies

Strategic planning is not entirely new to the higher education sector, though it is often confused with operational planning. Different forms of operational planning were common in British and Australian universities in the

1980s because their respective governments required targets to be established and met. The goal was to demonstrate efficiency gains (Robertson & Olds, 2018). Yet, as Clark (1998:p.5) noted, "traditional European universities have long exhibited a notoriously weak capacity to steer themselves. As their complexity has increased and the pace of change accelerated, that weakness has become more debilitating, deepening the need for a greater managerial capacity." If universities do not move beyond operational to strategic plans, it is unlikely that the needed changes to align with their future environments will occur (Crow & Dabars, 2015; Pritchard, 2018; Shin, 2017).

In many universities, a new strategy is published as a weighty document, which then collects dust on a president's bookshelf (Anderson, Johnson & Milligan, 1999). The consequences of dust-covered strategies are significant but invisible, including the sunk costs of the time, effort, and financial resources that went into their planning, compounded by a lack of preparation for the future. However, it is not just universities that fail to implement their strategy; business researchers have found that two-thirds to three-quarters of large organisations fail to implement their strategies (Sull, Homkes & Sull, 2015). When an institutional strategy does not move beyond a superficial response to external pressures, the results include underperforming initiatives and missed opportunities, as well as faculty and staff continuing to operate in their silos. It also reinforces an ongoing belief that a strategy is only window dressing, intended to satisfy the expectations of funders.

Complacency towards institutional strategies is also reinforced by a systemic belief that universities will not disappear because of their critical role in society (Pierce, 2017). This belief may have been valid in the previous century; however it parallels the five stages that many great companies move through. These are: (1) hubris born of success, (2) undisciplined pursuit of more, (3) denial of risk and peril, (4) grasping for salvation, and (5) capitulation to irrelevance or death (Collins, 2001). The relevance of Collins' (2001) phases to university leaders is illustrated in relabelling them to: (1) our university is critical to the community, (2) government and donors will continue to fund universities, (3) students will always need to be educated and our research is being published, so it must be relevant, (4) governments are no longer providing sufficient funds and donors are skeptical of how their money is being used, and (5) other institutions have more effective educational and research programmes.

The shift from Phase 3 to Phases 4 and 5 is becoming more visible in higher education because of a number of trends. Costs of a university education have become prohibitive, compounded by the increasing ability of students to develop skills independently from universities. Technology and regulatory changes are allowing non-academic competitors to provide credentials that reflect accomplishment of specific skill sets, without students having to incur the cost of a four-year degree (Christensen & Eyring, 2011; Smith, 2020). Ignoring disruptive trends and failing to implement strategies is not unique to universities. As Collins (2001) noted, decline sneaks up and then, seemingly all of a sudden, the organisation is unable to respond to changing demands. Preventing the last two phases of decline is difficult for universities without strategic plans to guide decision-making. Strategy researchers have noted that staying in the middle of the pack is a death-nail, yet many organisations choose the low risk/low performance middle ground (Raynor, 2007). This phenomenon is currently playing out in some jurisdictions, such as the United States, where institutions are being merged or closed as a result (Camera, 2019; Education Dive Staff, 2020).

Strategies also fail because they are linked to too many goals or inappropriately detailed plans. Researchers have found that many executives cannot provide a clear explanation of their organisation's strategy, and if they cannot describe it to their employees, it is unlikely to be implemented (Collis & Rukstad, 2008). A common assumption in strategic planning in universities is that multiple goals are needed to ensure that every unit on campus can identify with at least one or two. However, setting too many goals leads to confusion, partly because it is difficult to provide a simple explanation to justify them and the process to achieve them. A strategy should simplify decision-making by providing clarity on how individuals can structure their activities in support of two or three strategic goals (Burgelman, 2002; Vermeulen, 2017). The logic behind the strategy is as important as the goals because it provides the explanation for why changes are needed.

Failure also occurs because of insufficient communication. Once a strategy has been developed, its success is dependent on the initiatives of faculty and staff (Burgelman, 2002); thus it is critical that they understand how the strategy will lead to future success. A simple strategy, with two or three goals, is easy to communicate and provides continuous feedback on its progress, so faculty and staff feel valued for their contribution (Vermeulen, 2017). When they understand how their efforts, and the choices they make, contribute to the institution's strategic goals, they are more motivated to actively support the strategy. Strategies also fail when there is minimal communication on key performance indicators (KPIs) that reflect progress towards the strategic goals. When performance is not regularly measured and communicated to stakeholders, KPIs become invisible. Once that happens, accountability for strategic goals disappears and individuals establish their own priorities, reverting to a culture of silos.

Strategy as a Contract

When a new president[1] is appointed to lead a university, the first question stakeholders invariably ask is "What is your vision for the institution?" It is as if the president should show up on the first day with a fully developed plan, that resonates across a diverse set of constituents and magically propels the institution forward to new heights of success. Of course, this is not realistic and such an approach would very quickly land the new president in hot water.

Although the search process for a new president informs the incoming leader of areas of opportunity or growth, it does not replace the necessity for the president to lead the creation of a strategic plan that is developed through comprehensive stakeholder engagement. The mandate for new presidents, or those starting a second (or third) term, is often broadly defined by the board[2] at the start of their term. It may include such goals as: grow the student body, enhance the student experience, deepen relationships with external community partners, and increase research funding and impact. These goals may well end up in a strategic plan, but they do not create a vision or narrative for the future. And, they often do not reflect the result of rigorous vetting by stakeholders such as students, faculty, staff, alumni, and community leaders. By extension, the broad mandate set by the board may actually be at odds with what the community wants or expects, and it is risky for a president to initially assume that everyone is on the same page.

The development of a new institutional strategy creates an opportunity for engagement on campus and across the community, and it provides a unique platform for the president to meet and listen to a broad base of constituents in a quasi-structured environment. It also provides significant visibility, which can be invaluable to a new president in terms of signalling their leadership style and personal approach.

Perhaps the most important outcome of a strategic planning process for the president is that it creates a clear mandate for their tenure as leader of their institution. In essence, the strategic plan becomes an unwritten contract between the president, the board, and the community of stakeholders. It should be used by the board to evaluate the president's performance as a means of fulfilling their fiduciary duties around strategic oversight and as the basis for rewarding the president for delivering on the institution's strategic goals. These aspects are discussed further in Chapter 5.

One of the hardest aspects of any leadership role is managing expectations—those the leaders hold for themselves as well as from others. This is particularly true in the higher education sector due to the diverse and often contradictory views of stakeholders, as well as the lack of a clear bottom line. A well-designed and vetted strategic plan is a powerful tool to manage these conflicting expectations, as it provides a platform to link decisions (to do something or not do something) back to process, and a document based on input from a wide swath of stakeholders. Although this does not ensure that all stakeholders will be satisfied at all times, it provides a president with a mechanism, as well as courage and resolve, to demonstrate that they are acting in the best interests of the institution as a whole. At a minimum, it should give presidents the ability to sleep well at night.

Five-Phase Strategic Planning and Execution Process

There is no one right way to perform a strategic planning exercise. There are many pathways which can lead to an inspirational, broadly endorsed, and actionable strategy. In fact, the pathway—or journey—is the most important aspect of strategic planning since it plays a key role in determining the depth of engagement with stakeholders, the degree of rigour in assessing environmental trends and strategic options, as well as the ultimate level of commitment by the internal and external communities to the final strategic goals.

Prior to initiating the planning process, it is important to build agreement on the principles that will guide the process. These principles need to be public and visibly applied throughout the process as they establish both legitimacy of the process and trust that the process will lead to an effective strategy. Table 1.1 presents sample principles along with the goals to be achieved through their implementation (University of Calgary, 2016).

Table 1.1 Sample Principles to Guide the Strategic Planning Process

Goal: The strategic planning process should be:	*Principle:* The strategic planning process should ensure that:
Educational	• Internal and external stakeholders learn about external trends, internal strengths and limitations, and future opportunities for the institution
Inclusive	• Representatives from key internal and external stakeholders actively engage in, and contribute to, a respectful, transparent process
Collaborative and Consultative	• Engagement discussions are future-focused towards the good of the whole institution
Leveraged	• Appropriate university events are utilised to gather information and ideas
Inspirational	• Internal and external communities are invigorated and committed to the new or revised strategy for the institution

Although not every institution will adopt all of these principles, the one principle that should guide every consultation process is that it will be "educational." Consultation should be based on informed two-way exchanges, where participants have access to relevant background information on current programmes and trends prior to providing their thoughts and opinions on the institution's future programmes and direction. Informed participants can validate (or contradict) the impact of specific trends, provide differing interpretations of the institution's strengths and weaknesses, and substantiate any conclusions about current and desired future states. When the process is educational, individuals are better informed about why and how specific changes facilitate the university's progress towards a successful, sustainable future.

The activities needed to support effective planning and implementation of the strategy are illustrated in Table 1.2. These five phases provide a pathway from setting the stage for the strategic planning process, to fully operationalizing the plan through accountabilities, robust communication strategies, and an effective institutional culture to support transformational change.

Phase 1 (setting the stage) includes the work done prior to launching the formal stakeholder engagement process. The work in this phase, led by the president, includes communicating the rationale for a strategic planning process, reinforcing the value of stakeholder participation, ensuring the appropriate governance structure and resources are in place, and providing a timeline for the process and ultimate strategy launch. The outcome of this phase is a clear line-of-sight from start to end on the strategic planning activities and the approval structure for the final strategy (see Chapter 2).

The main purpose of Phase 2 (informed engagement) is to provide stakeholders with relevant background information so that they are aware of current programmes and processes as well as external trends and potential

Table 1.2 Five Phases for Strategic Planning and Execution in Higher Education

Phase 1: Setting the Stage	Phase 2: Informed Engagement	Phase 3: Creating the Strategy	Phase 4: Executing the Strategy	Phase 5: Future-Proofing
A. Dialoguing with stakeholders	A. Building an engagement platform	A. Developing the strategy	A. Converting strategy to operations	A. Communicating strategic impacts
B. Establishing legitimacy	B. Consulting with stakeholders	B. Building identity and awareness	B. Driving the operational plan	B. Enhancing an effective institutional culture

disruptors. It requires a comprehensive engagement platform for stakeholders to access documents and follow progress of the strategic planning
process. It also includes formal consultation processes which draw on stakeholder experience, expertise, and views of the future through structured (or
semi-structured) engagement (see Chapter 3).

Phase 3 involves developing the actual strategic plan, which involves
shifting the effort from gathering input through campus-wide stakeholder
engagement to a small working committee responsible for analysing and
interpreting the external and internal data. The focus is on integrating external risks and opportunities, and internal strengths and weaknesses into strategic opportunities, with a goal of consolidating around a strategic direction
that provides a future path for the institution. Once the strategy is developed,
it needs refinement through dialogue with stakeholders and approval by the
appropriate governance bodies. This is followed by the creation of an identity and formal launch to the community (see Chapter 4).

All of the important work in the first three phases establishes a new starting line for the execution of the strategy, which is the focus of Phase 4. Often
this phase is an afterthought for leaders as they assume everyone will just
get on with the job. This is a serious mistake since the strategy will not be
supported without an operational plan, which identifies priorities and establishes accountabilities and benchmarks (see Chapter 5).

The activities in Phase 5 focus on future-proofing by communicating the
intended strategic outcomes and impacts, as well as building and enhancing
an effective institutional culture to drive change and performance. When the
strategy becomes part of the "DNA" of the organisation, is it truly owned
and driven by the entire stakeholder community (see Chapter 6).

Summary

Universities are diffuse and complex, with diverse groups of stakeholders.
There will always be disagreement over the appropriate strategic priorities,
such as the allocation of resources to one of the pillars over the others; however, the probability of passive acceptance, rather than active resistance, is
increased if the logic behind the intended outcomes is communicated. The
key components to strategic success are the visibility of the strategic priorities, the logic behind the priorities, consistent decisions, and the evaluation
of progress towards the goals.

Academic institutions without strategic direction experience redundan-
cies and inefficiencies in resource allocation, systemic conflicts, and are
reactive rather than proactive to disruptions. Effective university strategies align and allocate resources through transparent decision-making for
recruitment, new programme development, research capacity growth, and

Table 1.3 Chapter Summary: Institutional Dynamics and the Role of Strategy

---

- Higher education is being disrupted through "massification" of education in some jurisdictions and contraction in others, the advent of new technologies, additional accountability requirements by funders, and the race for improved rankings to build perceived reputation and prestige.
- The internal dynamics of universities have been slow to change with faculty members, and some staff, operating in the silos of their department or discipline. As long as individuals have the resources they need there is little thought about institutional efficiency or overall effectiveness.
- Universities operate in unique contexts, with differing strengths, weaknesses, and potential to respond to opportunities and risks. A strategy is based on these unique contexts and states where a university should be in the future.
- An effective strategy leads to increased impact, which improves stakeholder satisfaction and institutional reputation. It reduces political conflicts and simplifies decision-making through visible priorities and by focusing attention on a limited number of strategic choices.
- Most strategic plans fail due to poor or limited execution. When a strategy never moves beyond a superficial response to external pressures, faculty and staff continue operating in their silos, leading to underperforming initiatives as well as missed opportunities.
- University leaders can manage competing views across multiple stakeholders when a strategy has been collectively developed and implemented. Strategic priorities reduce conflict, arising from competing views, by increasing transparency and consistency in the allocation of resources.
- A strategy creates a clear mandate and can serve as an unwritten contract between the president, the board, and the community of stakeholders. The board should use the strategic plan to fulfill their fiduciary duty of strategic oversight.
- The steps taken to develop a strategic plan play a key role in determining the depth of engagement with stakeholders, the degree of rigour in assessing environmental trends and strategic opportunities, and the commitment by the community to achieve the final strategic goals.

---

infrastructure investment. They can be a powerful tool to grow, reshape, or transform a university, while positively engaging and enabling key stakeholders in the process. They can build a stronger community, which constructively identifies with the institution, while still supporting faculties and units which have their own disciplinary needs or functional roles.

Table 1.3 provides a summary of the areas of discussion in this chapter.

Notes

1. President is used herein although the title of a university leader will vary between institutions and jurisdictions (e.g., president, president and vice-chancellor, vice chancellor, president and CEO, principal)
2. Board is used herein although it is recognised that the nomenclature for the institutional governing body varies between jurisdictions (e.g., board of governors, board of trustees)

2 Setting the Stage

Embarking on a strategic planning process presents an exciting opportunity for a president. It allows for aspirational thinking in the context of shaping and transforming the institution's future, while building resilience in an era of unprecedented change. A president is often eager to initiate a strategic planning process because it is a time of institutional renewal and a mechanism to translate aspirations and ideas into a concrete mandate for action. Two rationales for initiating a strategic planning process are timing and change of leadership. In terms of time, an existing strategic plan should be reviewed at regular intervals to ensure that there is continued alignment with evolving external trends and visible progress towards the established goals. Often, when a new leader is recruited to an institution, it is with an expectation that a new strategic plan will be a key deliverable during their initial mandate. Of course an externally recruited leader needs time to understand the institution's history, culture, people, programmes, and community. New leaders need to also determine where support for change and pockets of resistance are located across the institution. Hence, an external leader usually initiates a process within the first two years of their term, while internally recruited leaders may be in a position to initiate a strategic planning process earlier, since they are already familiar with the institution's history, culture, and operating environment.

Prior to launching a process, the president needs to understand the level of change and transformation required, and build trust with stakeholders to reduce the conventional inertia to change. Each group of stakeholders will be looking to the president to respond to a specific set of interests, and trust is built when a president is able to demonstrate an understanding of their needs. Once trust is formed, the legitimacy of the strategic planning process must be established through an inclusive and visible governance structure.

This chapter focuses on the early steps of building trust and establishing legitimacy, which are presented as Phase 1 in Table 2.1. Figure 2.1 lists the main activities of each step. Although they are presented in sequence, they

Table 2.1 Phase 1 of Five-Phase Strategic Planning Process

Phase 1: Setting the Stage	Phase 2: Informed Engagement	Phase 3: Creating the Strategy	Phase 4: Executing the Strategy	Phase 5: Future-Proofing
A. Dialoguing with stakeholders	A. Building an engagement platform	A. Developing the strategy	A. Converting strategy to operations	A. Communicating strategic impacts
B. Establishing legitimacy	B. Consulting with stakeholders	B. Building identity and awareness	B. Driving the operational plan	B. Enhancing an effective institutional culture

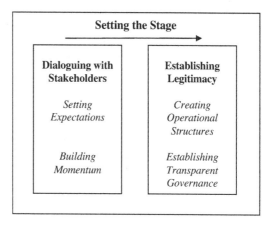

Figure 2.1 Components to Set the Stage

can be performed in parallel. If the stage is set appropriately, the outcome will be an informed and motivated institutional community energised to start formal strategic planning consultation, which is discussed in Chapter 3.

Dialoguing With Stakeholders

In this phase, a president's primary responsibilities are to build motivation and acceptance for a strategic planning process, and excitement about creating a vision of where the institution should be in five to 10 years. The primary actions in this early phase are listed in Table 2.2. Initial acceptance of the process is built through effective communication with five groups of stakeholders: the board, senior campus leaders, faculty, staff, and students.

Table 2.2 Dialoguing with Stakeholders

Actions	Outcome
• Visible leadership by the president to build awareness and create excitement for a new vision for the institution • Dialogue with key stakeholder groups on why a new strategy is needed and their role in engaging in the process	Informed and motivated institutional community

Initial conversations with students may include representatives from the broader student population and student leaders, some of whom may already be members of the board. Dialogue with faculty members may start with the academic senate and then broadened to be more inclusive of the entire academic community. An underlying assumption is that the president has already built consensus with their executive team—comprised of the provost and vice presidents—since their support and participation is critical to both the planning process and strategy execution (see Chapter 5).

Each of these groups has different concerns and interests, and the president should have a communication plan to ensure that the information needs of each group are satisfied, there are blocks of time for active listening, and the messages are both informative and inspirational. The messages need to be consistent, with their framing adjusted to ensure it is relevant to the particular group receiving the information. At all times the president should engage in an open-minded dialogue, as this is the initial opportunity for learning about unanticipated concerns or issues.

The board should be the first point of communication, since it is responsible for oversight of the institution's strategy. A new president may have a mandate to develop a new strategic plan; however, as previously noted, they need to gain familiarity with the campus and its institutional culture prior to discussions with the board on the level of change required and resources needed. In contrast, the discussions between a continuing president and board should cover whether the current strategy is directing the institution towards its anticipated future, trends have changed over the past five years, and visible progress towards the strategic goals is occurring. A key conversation point on the agenda should be the need for continual strategic renewal, involving campus-wide discussions on required changes in processes or programmes, so the institution is proactive in mitigating or adapting to potential disruptions.

Once the board and president agree on the need and purpose for the strategic planning process, it is important for the president to continue discussions on where the strategy should take the institution, and the board's role in approving and implementing the strategy. The involvement of the board in the strategic planning process is further discussed in the next chapter.

The president also needs to attend to the interests of senior campus leaders, such as deans, associate vice-presidents, and vice-provosts. This level of leadership is concerned with how the strategic planning process and its outcomes impact the allocation of resources, development and delivery of operational plans for their particular unit, and the role they are expected to play in the process. These stakeholders lead the different "silos" on campus, and as such, they are advocates for, and often fiercely protective of, their constituencies. In order to gain the support of these stakeholders a shared understanding of the positive impact that institutional growth and an improved reputation will have on each silo is needed. Thus, the president's message must consistently articulate the need for institutional-level planning while respecting the interests of individual faculties and units. These leaders are the main communication channels to their constituents, therefore their commitment influences the success of the strategic planning process and the plan itself. The role of the deans is particularly critical because of their perceived academic legitimacy and alignment with the needs of their faculty (Tierney & Lanford, 2018). An important component of the shared understanding between the president and deans is that a successful university is based on faculty strategic plans that are synergistic, and not competitive, with the institutional strategy. And, once the institutional strategy is developed faculty strategies should be refined or revised to align with it.

Once the president has built a consensus with the board, and ensured that senior campus leaders understand that the strategic planning process will elevate, not threaten, their areas, the president can go public and build support in the internal and external communities. This stage of communication does not require the same level of one-on-one conversations as with the previous two stakeholders. Messages about the upcoming planning processes can be integrated into existing events or new group discussion forums, such as town halls. External stakeholders are likely to be more accepting of the process than internal ones, so the president should focus on inspiring internal stakeholders through the building of future opportunities, as well as informing them of the process that will unfold.

Faculty and staff are normally concerned with how impending changes will influence their daily work and careers, and resist any suggestions coming from outside their silos (Chandler, 2013; Tagg, 2012). Their resistance arises from a number of factors, including the nature of a faculty's culture, protection of their discipline-based territory, frictions between functional divisions, resource allocation, traditions, leadership, communication, unions, and individual idiosyncrasies (Chandler, 2013). The reputation and impact of the institution is dependent on the work of its faculty. It is therefore critical that the president is aware of the basis of resistance and finds ways to increase openness to the strategic planning activities and their outcomes. Students are concerned with the need for quality academic programmes supported by a strong student experience. They are also focused on the financial investment and how the overall value of their educational experience prepares them for their futures.

During this early phase it is important to limit perceptions that the final strategy will be crafted by a privileged few. Thus, the message that broad engagement and consultation are critical in the development of an effective strategy, and that all stakeholders will be at the table, needs to be continually reinforced. Discussion of the details around consultation mechanisms should be limited because they could distract from the primary message of the need for broad engagement. In contrast, the president could provide opportunities for input on the strategic planning process. Maintaining an open approach at this stage should limit opportunities for the naysayers, who naturally gravitate to cynicism around strategic planning processes, to say "nobody asked me my opinion!"

Setting Expectations

A strategic planning process based on a completely blank strategy slate is rare and leads to confusion. An effective process requires boundaries and structure, and an understanding of the level of anticipated change needed. One of the implicit boundaries influencing strategy discussions is the university's unique history (Shin, 2017), while more visible boundaries are set by the president's insights and understanding of the level of change needed, and external and internal trends influencing the quality of the university's programmes. A university's history includes its mandate, relevant government regulations, sources of funding, and alumni experiences. Usually a president's insights are gained through the onboarding process (if new in the position), previous leadership experiences, a review of the current context of the university, and overall knowledge of the higher education sector. There may also be external contexts that are particularly important to a region—such as supporting Indigenous students and communities—that should be woven into the consideration of change required.

The president will also have a sense of the level of change needed to align the university with its future external environment. They have knowledge, via their networks and institutional planning staff, of the broad trends influencing higher education, including best practices in other institutions, government expectations or accountabilities, academic and research plans, and institutional reports. Each institution is impacted by a unique combination of internal and external factors, which influences the level of change needed by the institution's strategy (Shin, 2017). Table 2.3 lists factors which influence the magnitude of strategic change needed.

Although an ongoing assumption is that a new strategic plan should deliver transformative impact, this is not always an appropriate goal. As noted in Table 2.3, the level of strategic change ranges from incremental to transformative; prior to initiating the strategic planning process a president should be in a position to understand where the university falls on this continuum of change. It could be argued that organisational evolution is a normal progression, and, when only incremental changes are required, it is unnecessary to spend resources and time on a strategic planning process. However, this assumption can lead to complacency and missed opportunities. A strategic planning process focused on identifying needed incremental changes creates additional value by reinforcing and reinvigorating both the direction and priorities of the existing plan, and an effective institutional culture which integrates the campus silos through a unifying vision.

Table 2.3 Factors Influencing the Level of Strategic Change Needed

Environment \ Level of Change	Incremental	Transformational
Internal	• Priorities identified but no coherent overall strategy • Budgets support priorities but clear incentives lacking • Institutional metrics are being satisfied but are not ambitious	• Lack of a unifying direction • No clear priorities • Resources are not used to drive clear outcomes • Institutional units operate as silos
External	• Relatively stable funding sources • Technical advances are being continuously adopted • Reputation is reinforced with innovative programmes • Some community support through engagement and philanthropy	• Funding sources are unpredictable or declining • Technical advances will be disrupting status quo • Programmes are not aligned with community needs • Institution is not differentiated amongst peers • External collaborations are weak • Reputation is lagging expectations

Once the president has identified the level of change needed, the next step is to build a consensus with the board and senior leaders as to the outcomes of the strategic planning process. It is important to establish this consensus prior to the initiation of the strategic planning process because the anticipated level of change influences the resources and time committed to the strategic planning process, along with perceptions of its success. When the line-of-sight between resources and expected outcomes is clear, there is a shared appetite for the changes the new strategy will require, including the potential reallocation of resources, attraction of new resources, changes in personnel, new programme development, and elimination of initiatives.

At this point the president must strike a balance between offering ideas that garner excitement and stoke the possibilities for the future, and appearing to have already locked in strategic options. Although the president and senior leaders may have a good sense of the level of change needed, they should be prepared for input from stakeholders that may shift the resulting strategic plan to being more or less transformative than originally anticipated.

Building Momentum

The discussion so far has focused on the strategic aspects of the president's initial assessment of needed change; however, another critical responsibility is creating excitement about the process. It is part of the president's role to elevate the ambition of faculty and staff to an aspirational level, stretching views of what is potentially achievable through collective commitment. They need to instill hope, pride, and an openness to change. In order to build the trust necessary to implement the new strategy, the president needs to communicate respect for the time and emotions that individuals will commit when they participate in the process. Pierce (2017) discusses four academic institutions that had impactful strategic plans, and noted that a commonality across them was "planning was simultaneously aspirational and feasible, ultimately mediating between the real and the ideal."

Stakeholders want to know early in the strategic planning process how long it will take from beginning to end. This information is an implicit signal of the participative nature of the process, and allows stakeholders to anticipate their own involvement and when investments of their time will be required. Although the exact timing of each phase will not be known during initial communications, the president can provide an estimated length of time for the entire process, which is often eight to 12 months. Maintaining a sense of urgency and excitement during the consultation and strategy development stages is important, and this grows more challenging the longer the process. An extended timeframe for the process leads to diminishing and potentially negative returns.

The duration of the first phase may range from several weeks to months, according to each institution's operating context, including the impact of factors such as the existing culture, outcome of previous strategies, influence of current or anticipated trends, or reactions of key stakeholder groups. This phase should not be condensed since it is one of the most influential in terms of receptivity to the planning process. It not only builds legitimacy of the process, it is also the first step in establishing trust and an enhanced institutional culture.

Overall, preparation of the campus for the strategic planning process should engage all of the key stakeholder groups including students, faculty, staff, alumni, community leaders, and donors. Government personnel, including elected officials and bureaucrats (i.e., municipal, provincial/state, or federal) are also important stakeholders as they can provide feedback on their priorities. It is crucial that the president be—and be seen to be—leading this discussion and be fully committed to the process, the final strategic plan, and critically, its implementation.

Establishing Legitimacy

Legitimacy of a strategic planning process is difficult to establish at most universities, given the "organised chaos" in higher education. The president's creation of a genuine dialogue with stakeholders around the need and opportunity for a new strategic plan is a critical first step to mitigate concerns. A second step is establishing visible structures to reinforce the message that the strategic planning process is campus wide (and beyond) and transparent. This is particularly important for faculty and staff, who operate in the various silos on campus.

Table 2.4 lists the actions to establish the legitimacy of the strategic planning process. Although many people are involved in setting up the strategic and operational oversight of the process and outcomes, the president needs to provide visible leadership on developing the governance structures since it is a campus-wide process with significant impacts on the future of the institution.

Table 2.4 Establishing Legitimacy

Actions	Outcome
• Creation of operational structure that ensures broad stakeholder representation and process efficiency • Establishment of a transparent governance process for decision-making and approvals	Accepted legitimacy of the strategic planning process

Creating Operational Structures

The operational structure for the strategic planning process should be simple and coherent, while creating a line-of-sight between stakeholders and the strategy. A simple structure includes a strategic oversight committee to oversee the process and outcomes, and a working committee to conduct and manage the activities that need to be completed at each stage.

Membership of the strategic oversight committee should reflect the broad constituents of the institution including faculty, staff, administrators, students, alumni, and the board, as well as the community, and may reach a membership of 10 to 15 people. The committee's main responsibilities are to provide oversight of the design and implementation of the communications strategy and consultation process, in addition to reviewing feedback themes, document drafts, and the final strategy document prior to submission to the formal governance process for approval.

The strategic oversight committee serves three main purposes. First, it provides a voice at the table for all key stakeholder representatives in the moulding of the process and final strategy. Second, it provides a communication channel from each stakeholder representative to their constituents to keep them informed of the progress. Third, it increases the legitimacy of the strategic planning process by creating a link between the oversight committee and the institution's governance bodies (academic senate and board), reducing potential concerns that the strategic planning process is operating outside of accepted institutional decision-making structures. A strategic oversight committee, with representative membership and monitoring rather than operational responsibilities, satisfies both legitimacy and efficiency interests.

Selection of a chair for the oversight committee involves political as well as strategic factors. The president should chair the committee if they want active engagement in the final outcome and processes, while also maintaining visible independence from the consultation activities. However, if there is the potential for perceptions of the president having undue control, a highly trusted faculty member (or a few faculty members) can be appointed as chair (or co-chairs). Under this option it is important that the chair has a strong reputation across multiple constituency groups, and a solid working relationship with the president.

To be effective, the working committee should be composed of campus leaders and strategy experts who have a high level of credibility on campus and deep knowledge of the institution and its culture, as well as strong project management skills. This committee is responsible for the day-to-day operations, design, structuring, and implementation of the consultation activities, analysis of the results, and preparation of the initial strategy documents for review.

Membership of the working committee should be relatively small, ensuring it is nimble and well coordinated; typically it will have four to seven people. Given the level of work required, the members should either be wholly seconded to the strategic planning process, or have the work assigned as a large component of their responsibilities during that time. They should also have the authority to draw on other staff and the necessary resources to perform the required work. One member of the committee should be from the president's office so there is an ongoing and direct linkage to the president.

Consultants can be retained to do the heavy lifting for the working committee. There are a number of consulting firms with teams who have strong insights into strategic planning processes and specialise in the higher education sector. Leveraging their national or global expertise can save time by providing valuable comparator information and access to networks. The concerns associated with consultants include additional cost and a belief amongst some stakeholders (faculty being at the top of the list) that they are being managed by people who do not understand the uniqueness of their institution and its culture.

Alternatively, many institutions have internal capacity to do a lot of the day-to-day work—both operational and strategic. The advantage of this approach is that internal faculty and administrators have a strong knowledge of the institution and—if selected properly—existing credibility with stakeholders. For example, most institutions have internal planning groups (sometimes called institutional analysis) as well as strategy experts who are often in the business school. Whether external or internal consultants, or a combination of the two, are used, the working committee must own the process in terms of tracking documents, drafting reports, developing communications materials, coordinating and conducting the consultation process, and monitoring timelines as discussed in later chapters.

Establishing Transparent Governance

In order to establish a transparent governance process for decision-making and approvals, the institution's key governance bodies are utilised to maintain an alignment to existing approval processes. Specific responsibilities for these bodies vary according to the legislation or charter under which the institution operates. The academic senate and board should approve the terms of reference for the strategic oversight committee, which define its mandate, membership, and responsibilities. These bodies should also engage in the consultation process, review and provide feedback on drafts of the strategic plan, and approve the final strategic plan document.

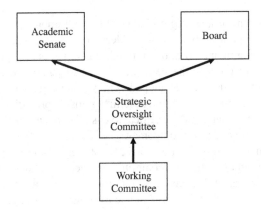

Figure 2.2 Strategic Planning Governance Structure

Figure 2.2 depicts a relatively simple governance structure for the strategic planning process. Although the president is not specifically shown in the figure, in most institutions they are a member of both the academic senate and the board. As discussed earlier in this chapter, they may also be a member of the strategic oversight committee, and if not, it is expected that they work closely with the chair to maintain a high level of coordination.

The final task of this phase is to establish and map out the activities, timeline, and budget for the entire strategic planning process. This includes all of the activities from the time the president starts preparing the campus to the launching of the strategic plan, and should also include milestones, timing of resource allocation (e.g., people, funding, physical spaces, contractors), and deliverables. This should be mapped out by the working committee, reviewed by the strategic oversight committee, and approved by the president or board depending on resources required. A timeline serves as a concrete measure of progress in relation to the prepared schedule of deliverables; it increases the coordination of work between the oversight and working committees, and provides metrics to communicate to the campus on the progress made. It also provides campus planners sufficient time to identify where resource constraints may impact the process, since on-time achievement of deliverables reinforces the legitimacy of the process. All information can be collocated into a project management tool in order to monitor progress and timelines so deadlines are clear and tracked.

Summary

The development of a strategic plan to guide and transform an institution is an exciting opportunity for stakeholders to work together as a community to articulate their aspirations through a comprehensive process. Prior to launching this process, the stage must be set so stakeholders understand why a strategy needs to be developed, who will be engaged, and when the consultation process will begin. These first steps of preparing the campus are led by the president, and are critical to ensure that stakeholders will support both the process and its outcomes.

In addition, the infrastructure to drive the strategic planning process must be established in the form of a committee to oversee the design and implementation of a stakeholder consultation process as well as the development of the strategic plan itself. This strategic oversight committee is populated

Table 2.5 Chapter Summary: Setting the Stage

- A president sets the stage before the formal consultation process by engaging in genuine dialogue with stakeholders to build motivation and acceptance for a strategic planning process and excitement towards a future vision.
- The board is responsible for oversight of the institutional strategy. A shared understanding between the president and board of why a new strategy is needed, where it should take the institution, and how the board will be involved in the process is important.
- A president builds trust with campus leaders by articulating the need for institutional-level planning while respecting individual faculties. The role of a faculty plan relative to the institutional plan needs to be seen as synergistic and not competitive.
- Building support for a strategic planning process in the broader external community is critical. External stakeholder focus should be on inspiring them about future opportunities.
- Internal stakeholders have concerns about the impact of impending changes, so the president must emphasise that an institutional plan provides a platform to consolidate their ambitions in a unified strategic direction to increase opportunities for additional impacts.
- The president builds a common understanding with the board and senior leaders by setting expectations on whether the strategic plan should lead to transformational change for the university or whether incremental change is in order.
- To establish legitimacy, a simple operational structure is used. A strategic oversight committee, with broad constituent representation, oversees the process and outcomes, while a working committee conducts and manages the day-to-day activities.
- To establish a transparent governance process for decision-making and approvals, key governance bodies are used to maintain alignment to existing processes. The academic senate and board approve the final strategic plan.

---

with representatives of key constituencies. A smaller working committee of resource personnel and experts drives the process and manages day-to-day activities. Although these committees perform the work needed to develop the strategic plan on behalf of the institution, the actual approval of the final strategy is usually done by the key governance bodies, namely the academic senate and the board.

Table 2.5 provides a summary of key points in the "setting the stage" phase.

3 Informed Engagement

Strategy-oriented engagement is a two-way information exchange, where campus leaders, faculty and staff share information related to their work and understanding of the future. Campus leaders monitor external trends, interact with a broad range of stakeholders, and have knowledge of the institution's overall operations; whereas faculty and staff have limited time and resources to monitor the broader environment, and often have minimal knowledge of cross-campus issues. This group does, on the other hand, have intimate knowledge of front-line university culture, and academic trends and needs. Other stakeholders, such as students, alumni, and community leaders, generally have limited familiarity with opportunities and potential disruptive trends.

Effective stakeholder consultation creates structured opportunities for all parties to develop a more informed perspective of the future higher education environment and where institutional change is required. It also provides platforms for constructive debate and input. In particular, it is important that faculty—given their independent focus and their expectations of being consulted on key decisions—have an opportunity to fully engage in the process. Faculty are the primary group influencing the university's reputation, and without their active support strategic plans will not succeed (Goldman & Salem, 2015).

Informed engagement requires participants to have an understanding of the broader external trends in order to effectively predict their impact on the university and their own work. Thus, a critical part of the engagement process is access to information on external trends and opportunities, higher education best practices, and internal strengths and limitations. With this information participants can validate or contradict the impact of specific trends, provide differing interpretations of the institution's strengths and weaknesses, and substantiate any conclusions about current and desired future states. A key principle of the strategic planning process is that an engagement platform will only be effective if all stakeholders have equal access to the same information.

Effective stakeholder engagement methods are future-oriented and structured to limit discussion of perceived past mistakes or unfairness. If grievances need to be aired, this should be done through alternative forums. Given the expectations of students, faculty, and staff the consultation activities need to be inclusive and collaborative, and align with the principles in Table 1.1. If the engagement activities are based on informed and future-oriented discussions, the outcome will be a collective understanding and support of the changes needed to ensure that the institution has a sustainable future.

This chapter focuses on building an effective and informed engagement process with a broad range of stakeholders, with the main steps highlighted as Phase 2 in Table 3.1. Discussions are further divided into four components as depicted in Figure 3.1. The combination of these components leads

Table 3.1 Phase 2 of Five-Phase Strategic Planning Process

Phase 1: Setting the Stage	*Phase 2: Informed Engagement*	*Phase 3: Creating the Strategy*	*Phase 4: Executing the Strategy*	*Phase 5: Future-Proofing*
A. Dialoguing with stakeholders	A. Building an engagement platform	A. Developing the strategy	A. Converting strategy to operations	A. Communicating strategic impacts
B. Establishing legitimacy	B. Consulting with stakeholders	B. Building identity and awareness	B. Driving the operational plan	B. Enhancing an effective institutional culture

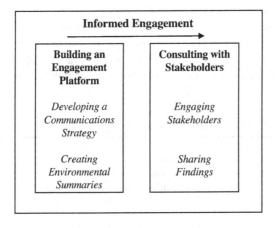

Figure 3.1 Components to Support Informed Engagement

participants to understand why change is needed and how they can contribute to the institution's strategic goals. Different tools to maximise constructive and future-oriented discussions are described in the following sections.

Building an Engagement Platform

Most faculty and staff are reluctant to participate in activities that are not directly linked to their individual career success; thus the strategic planning process must be viewed as an authentic step towards improving the sustainability of both the university and the individual's work. Researchers have found that faculty are more likely to participate in strategic planning when they believe their involvement is valued and that the activities are structured and informative (Adewale & Esther, 2012; Thompson, 2017). Their motivation to participate is influenced by regular communications that reinforce the importance of the engagement processes in shaping the institutional strategy, easy access to relevant information influencing the need for strategic changes, and coordinated and intentional engagement activities. All three of these actions should be managed through an engagement platform as shown in Table 3.2.

Developing a Communications Strategy

A communications strategy should include the following components: branding of the strategic planning process to increase awareness, working through multiple communication channels—traditional and digital—to reach a broad range of stakeholders, providing a website for coordinating participation and findings, and scheduling regular touchpoints with campus members. Communications about the strategic planning process should also be built into established ongoing campus and external activities.

The communication process should begin as soon as the legitimacy of the process is established in the "setting the stage" phase (Chapter 2), and continue past the launch of the strategy documents. Starting communications

Table 3.2 Building an Engagement Platform

Actions	Outcome
• Execution of a comprehensive communications strategy that creates awareness and inspires stakeholders • Development of environmental summaries based on an analysis of external trends and internal capacities	Maximised informed stakeholder participation in formal consultation

Table 3.3 Examples of Communication Strategy Components

Communication Components	Sample Activities
Branding	• Build awareness and reinforce importance through a brand (i.e., colour, logo) • Use brand in social media, posters, T-shirts
Multiple Channels	• Use of a range of channels for updates about what is happening via newsletters, e-mails, social media
Website	• Create a constant location to obtain organisation information, background summaries, and working papers
Simple Options	• Use weekly questions or polls to gather opinions on strategic concerns with regular feedback
Integration	• Leverage existing communication channels by building messages into other campus initiatives
Toolkits	• Provide campus leaders with messages, core slide decks, and tools to increase interest in the process

prior to the actual engagement processes builds momentum and sends an implicit message that participation is valued. One of the goals of the communications strategy should be the consistent messaging that future-proofing of the institution can only be accomplished through a strategic planning process that integrates university-wide contributions. Table 3.3 lists some examples of communication components.

Institutional leaders should be accountable for encouraging participation in their units. Starting with the president, campus leaders need to support the strategic planning process and communicate that it is underway, as well as champion its importance to their constituents. Leaders, at all levels, can champion the process by participating in a focus group, using their own social media channels, discussing engagement opportunities at team meetings (showing a core slide deck), putting a poster on their office door, and advocating the completion of an online survey.

Creating Environmental Summaries

Ensuring participants have access to high-quality information provides the opportunity for stakeholders at all levels of the university to better understand the institution's challenges and participate in thoughtful, effective discussions (Pierce, 2017). It also increases the validity of interpretations and conclusions on the impact of external trends on the institution. Two types of environmental scans inform the strategic planning process: one of internal

Table 3.4 Information Sources for Environmental Summaries

Internal Documents: Meso-Level Data	External Documents: Macro-Level Data
Strategic	Government
• institutional and faculty strategic plan(s)	• legislative reviews
• institutional reports and fact books	• government reports
• annual community reports	• budget documents
Operational	• funding formulas
• academic and research plans	• upcoming changes in legislation and plans
• enrolment and programme plans	
• workforce plans	Trends
• financial and capital plans	• economic and labour market forecasts
• governance structures	• higher education policies
Culture/Student Experience	• consortia shared data
• student satisfaction surveys	• higher education reports
• programme completion data	• geopolitical events
• student employment data	• demographic
• faculty and staff engagement surveys	• technical applications
External Stakeholder	• media and telecommunications
• reputational surveys	Best Practices
• alumni feedback	• contact with peer institutions
• donor feedback	• higher education research journals
	• university and college associations

documents providing meso-level data, and one of external trends providing macro-level data. Table 3.4 lists various information sources that can be used as inputs to these two environmental scans. Participants will not have time to read all documents in Table 3.4, thus summaries need to be developed by institutional planners or the working committee with minimal interpretation. These summaries should be reviewed by the strategic oversight committee for any biases that might have intentionally shaped them.

A summary of the internal environment should provide information on progress towards current goals, levels of stakeholder satisfaction, and the state of institutional resources, including finances, technical capacity, infrastructure, and staffing levels. Information on the effectiveness of research and teaching programmes should be provided through external objective measures (e.g., web of science indicators, rankings of academic programmes). The summary should contain sufficient information for participants to develop a relatively informed assessment of the efficiency and effectiveness of internal support for the delivery of programmes. Although much of the summarised information directly influences the work of faculty and staff and impacts students, it is not normally provided, or viewed, in a relatively concrete, holistic format. Thus, participants will have formed assumptions on the basis of their experience, within the silo they are working, and will not have a complete understanding of the internal factors influencing the institution's overall performance. The format of the internal scan can vary, with one option being three separate summaries, one for each pillar: teaching, research, and community engagement. Each one should delve into relevant trends that could impact activities within the pillar, review best practices, and highlight the status of programmes using quantitative data and qualitative discussions.

Regular scans of trends in the external environment are common within larger universities, with the results shared amongst the president and senior leaders. Trend data on political opinions and policies, economic developments, and demographics is often obtained from external specialists or reports. However, the interpretation of trends needs to be relative to the institution, since their impact varies with the unique context of each university, including its size, surrounding community, financial resources, and reputation.

An analysis of external political factors comprises a broad range of factors, including the government's orientation to higher education and public resource allocation, taxation on philanthropic donations, and policy reviews. Policy reviews contain important information about a government's outlook on the expected rate of economic growth, the long-term stability of local communities, and labour market forecasts. Geopolitical factors include potential global activities that could influence enrolments or specific research programmes. Socio-cultural factors include dimensions such as demographic trends, indigenisation, stakeholder expectations, and community dynamics. A review of emerging technologies should identify their potential disruption in specific research areas, academic programmes, and efficiencies of operational processes. Emerging technologies also act as signals to other sources of potential change.

University operations are influenced by health and safety, and anti-discrimination and employment regulations. Reviewing trends in media and telecommunications can improve the understanding of how people send and receive information to learn about the world and connect with each other, and what research or academic programmes are needed to build capacity or prepare students. Additional monitoring of environmental issues can increase an understanding of the local, national, or global issues requiring new research or academic programmes (e.g., including changes in climate and variations in resource consumption). Lastly, monitoring public health issues leads to a better understanding of potential changes in lifestyles, popular culture, and disease control that will influence the health of surrounding communities, enrolments and need for future programmes (Webb, 2020).

Minimal interpretation should be applied to the external information so individuals can form or adapt their own views. A PESTLE (i.e., political, economic, socio-cultural, technological, legislative, and environmental) framework categorises external trends according to their source, rather than interpreting them (e.g., threats or opportunities). Variations on the PESTLE approach have also been used by higher education institutional planners, such as STEEP (social, technology, economic, environment, political) which has an environmental dimension (SCUP, 2020). The impact of any one trend may be obvious: the more difficult analysis is identifying the interactions of the trends and their influence on operations or the feasibility of programmes.

The summaries should be available to stakeholders via the strategic planning website, which also reinforces the messages of transparency and valued participation. These summaries play an important role after the strategy has been implemented, in that they provide a calibration of the current operating context, and a baseline to measure the impact of the impending new strategy over the near to medium term. Thus, the website should be a repository of information that educates the campus, facilitates informed engagement, and provides benchmarks to assess progress towards the final strategic goals.

Consulting With Stakeholders

Each institution has its own combination of stakeholders interested in its future; a comprehensive consultation process, involving multiple access points, allows any interested stakeholder the option to participate. Similarly, once the consultation feedback is received, it needs to be aggregated and communicated back to participants as part of the commitment to transparency. These two actions—consultation and feedback—are listed in Table 3.5 and underpin a high-impact process that captures the complexity of the university's programmes and provides a foundation for strategy development, which is further discussed in Chapter 4.

Table 3.5 Consulting with Stakeholders

Actions	Outcome
• Design and implementation of a broad stakeholder engagement process using multiple engagement methods • Transparent feedback of consultation findings to stakeholder community	High-impact stakeholder consultation and feedback

Engaging Stakeholders

Stakeholders vary in the quality of their contributions to the strategic planning process. Some are constrained by time while others are only indirectly committed to the institution. Including stakeholders who have minimal time or commitment to understanding the current context requires additional filters during data analysis to ensure outlier data is recognised and interpreted as such. Although there is significant variation in the quality of contributions, the process needs to be inclusive to limit any perceptions of unfairness or defensiveness to criticism. There are a range of engagement activities that vary in terms of resource requirements and value or impact of information acquired (see Table 3.6); a combination of these activities can optimise the time and effort directed to engagement activities. In this table, stakeholders are categorised into primary and secondary, and the engagement methods are classified according to the quality of information, or impact, that is likely to be received from the method. Generally, high-impact activities require upfront time and expertise to develop appropriate group tasks or questionnaires, along with the formats for collecting and interpreting participant feedback. Low-impact activities are less focused on the quality of the information gathered and more on creating awareness of the process.

Faculty and staff have the capacity to contribute informed opinions, and those who choose to participate have a high level of commitment to the institution's future. Faculty are important as they are the stakeholders who deliver the mandate of the institution via their teaching, research, and service activities. Staff provide the essential services that support faculty and student outcomes. Leaders of both academic and non-academic units often

Table 3.6 Examples of Stakeholder Engagement Methods

Stakeholder Group	Stakeholder	Engagement Method (H/M/L)*
Primary (Internal)	Faculty	Focus Groups (H)
	Staff	Online Surveys (H)
	Internal Leaders	Town Halls (M)
	Board	Internal Forums (M)
	Students	E-mail and Web input (M)
		Roving Booths (L)
		Exhibits and Events (L)
Secondary (External)	Alumni	Focus Groups (H)
	Community Leaders	Roundtables (H)
	Partners	Online Surveys (M)
	Donors	Exhibits and Events (L)
	Government	Open Houses (L)

* H = High-impact activity; M = Medium-impact activity; L = Low-impact activity

have macro-level knowledge of institutional constraints and strengths, and are needed as champions of the consultation process. Members of the board provide valuable information about community expectations for the institution. Students—both undergraduate and graduate—are important internal stakeholders since they are the primary consumers of the institution's programmes and activities, and have expectations as to what skills and knowledge they need for their futures. There are specific communities—such as Indigenous and other racialized stakeholders—where outreach and engagement for dialogue and feedback is important to ensure diverse perspectives are heard. In addition, extra consideration needs to be given when an underrepresented stakeholder group does not have adequate access to the engagement opportunities listed in Table 3.6. In this case, alternative methods such as one-on-one or small group meetings may be required. Overall, internal engagement for the purpose of strategic planning should be focused on the primary stakeholder groups who have a direct influence on the implementation of identified changes, or are directly influenced by the strategic outcomes.

Although classified as a secondary group, external stakeholders provide valuable insights and a realistic grounding to the future due to their experiences outside the walls of the institution. Additionally, they influence the execution of the strategy by employing graduates, partnering with university faculty and programmes, and providing philanthropic investments. As such, they also act as informal ambassadors. For these reasons, the selection of external stakeholders is a sensitive and important task; it should be based not just on their credentials, but more importantly on their willingness to commit time and effort to understanding the institution's current context, and their knowledge of external trends.

It could be argued that there is minimal value in conducting low-impact engagement activities, given they do not lead to substantive input. However, each activity drives different outcomes, and when combined they facilitate a comprehensive view of the landscape. As an example, roving booths are stations set up at various locations on campus, with volunteers (e.g., students or staff) posing questions to passersby about their campus experience and recording the answers on a digital device. This method collects information low in relevance and validity for strategy development; nonetheless, the booths are justified due to the awareness they create of the strategic planning process. In contrast, informal round table discussions minimise resource requirements in terms of preparation and have a lower probability of gathering relevant information. However, they may be appropriate for external stakeholders, such as key leaders or donors who do not have time to prepare for more structured discussions. These individuals can still provide valuable information about community expectations for the institution through less structured processes. An effective engagement strategy aligns the specific method with the anticipated information, time, and commitment of a group of stakeholders, as well as ensuring that a wide range of stakeholders participate in the engagement activities. Integrating a broad range of engagement activities into the overall process leads to inclusivity and awareness.

A principle that should be applied to all engagement activities is that discussions are future-oriented. A natural tendency in giving feedback is to concentrate on complaints about historical events, under the assumption that the leadership should be correcting the situation. However, focusing on past or current perceived inequities reinforces the status quo rather than identifying changes needed for future sustainability. Thus, gathering information relevant to an institution's strategy requires structured and intentional engagement methods directed towards identifying the changes needed for the future. When discussion is structured appropriately, focus groups and surveys lead to relevant and effective recommendations for change, and a shift from potential complacency to a commitment to a new direction.

A consideration when preparing for the high impact engagement processes is whether an application for research ethics approval is required. This is an important step if there is potential that the data gathered during the engagement activities will be used by researchers. Whether or not research ethics approval is required and obtained, conventional informed consent practice, including guarantees of anonymity and confidentiality, should be followed prior to the focus groups and completion of online surveys.

Focus Group Discussions

One of the most effective high-impact engagement activities is structured group discussions because of their two-way exchange of information. When structured appropriately leaders learn about why programmes are effective or not, and participants gain an understanding of limitations and opportunities, as well as the trade-offs required to increase the future relevance and sustainability of institutional initiatives. Numerous articles describe how to structure and conduct effective focus group discussions (e.g., Parker & Tritter, 2006) and basic guidelines are listed in Table 3.7. Although the discussion in this table assumes that participants are meeting face to face, virtual focus groups can also be effectively held using online meeting platforms.

A useful organisation of large group discussions is to move through three phases: introduction, small group break-out, and large group debrief. The introductory phase includes all participants and covers the purpose of the session, the need for future-oriented discussions, direction on how to conduct the strategy exercise, and the requirement to conclude the small group work with three recommendations to share in the third-phase debrief.

Table 3.7 Guidelines for Structuring Effective Focus Group Strategy Discussions

Notification and Preparation
- Notifications are sent sufficiently ahead to allow individuals to clear their calendars
- Multiple focus group discussions are held on a range of topics
- Individuals choose which group discussion/topic they will join
- Individuals are provided environmental summary documents to prepare for the focus group

Organisation of Session
- Focus group sessions start and end on time, regardless of situational constraints
- A focus group session lasts between 60 and 90 minutes
- Focus group sessions have between 20 and 60 participants
- Small group discussions, within the session, have 10 or fewer participants
- Strategy tools are used to ensure that the discussion is focused on where the institution should be headed and the needed changes to reach the desired state
- Time is spent in small group discussions, with introduction and closure in large group

Conclusion of Session
- Each focus group reports three recommendations to the larger group debrief
- Conclusions or recommendations are recorded and posted on a website

After the introductory phase, participants move into small groups and are given an assigned question to be answered using the strategy exercise. The question should be framed to identify potential changes within a programme or pillar (teaching, research, or community engagement). After deliberating, each small group presents its three recommendations to the larger group. A limit of three recommendations forces each small group to identify areas of consensus and differences, and to establish priorities. If a limit is not set on the number of recommendations, group discussions can become a long list of issues, with participants not having to consider priorities. Not all groups reach a consensus, and some groups will conclude with conflicting recommendations. However, valuable information is still obtained when a group lacks agreement, as it provides an understanding of conflicting priorities on the campus, and why there is a lack of consensus. It also provides information about where additional communication may be needed when the strategy is launched.

The website should provide individuals a choice of focus group session topics (e.g., student experience, teaching, or research), the relevant environmental summaries for background preparation, and the session times and locations. A focus group session may cover a combination of topics, with the small group discussions directed towards issues relevant to one of the three pillars or specific programmes. A multi-topic session, where small group discussions cover issues in different pillars, has the benefit of participants learning about the need for change in areas where they were less informed. In general, stakeholders should have the option to sign up for any particular topic they choose; however, for some of the small group discussions, participation may be restricted to representatives from specific groups. For example, students who want to discuss topics relevant to "student experience" or "academic programmes" could choose "student only" or "student/faculty" groups. For the research pillar it may be beneficial to have some of the groups composed of only faculty researchers and administrative staff, while others may combine graduate students, faculty, and staff.

The primary outcome of a focus group session is the recording of three recommendations from each small group which, when aggregated with all of the feedback from the small groups in a large focus group session, provides a valuable summary. The recommendations are a critical source of data for the final gap analysis discussed in Chapter 4. Successful focus group discussions are a result of good facilitation. Skilled facilitators are able to manage the strategy exercises, effectively limit the airing of grievances, and seamlessly move between small and large group discussions. They are also able to build a sense of inclusiveness, ensure respect is given to all group members, particularly if controversial discussions develop, and manage time. Finally, they continuously reflect an objective listening orientation, without overlaying their personal opinions.

There are a variety of exercises that can be used to structure focus group discussions. The authors adapted two used in business consulting—the "strategy canvas" and the "eliminate-reduce-raise-create (ERRC) grid"—to guide focus groups within the higher education sector (Kim & Mauborgne, 2005). These exercises have been used across several institutions with positive feedback, as measured by effective group discussions and the provision of the appropriate information needed by strategy planners. The main difference between the two exercises is that strategy canvases are built by comparing their institution to others to identify where changes are needed, while the ERRC grid focuses on a review of internal factors to identify needed adjustments.

The strategy canvas was developed to identify market niches, called "blue oceans," where companies can establish a competitive advantage through a unique product or service (Kim & Mauborgne, 2005). Although academic institutions do not operate within the same context as businesses, the strategy canvas model can be adapted to identify opportunities to both enhance current programmes and create new initiatives within a higher education framework. A "blue ocean" can be thought of as a "sweet spot" of programmes or expertise, which differentiates the institution from its peers. This concept is further discussed in Chapter 4.

A strategy canvas is both a diagnostic and an action framework; it captures how other organisations are responding to disruptive trends and what programmes or attributes are valued by stakeholders (Kim & Mauborgne, 2005). It visualises the multiple perspectives of focus group participants by organising them into a descriptive graph. An important element of a strategy canvas is that it captures perceptions of participants and not hard data. Strategy canvases facilitate collaborative conversations where ideas are shared, with some dropped and others kept, and to reach conclusions about needed changes.

Each strategy canvas is developed around a question such as, "What factors need to be adjusted to improve teaching and learning activities so in five years students can satisfy their educational needs?" Or for a group of science professors, the question might be more specific: "What factors will optimise student skills development in science-based programmes in five years?"

The question is answered by comparing the institution to two or three other universities on selected factors. These factors may be prescribed by the facilitator or they may be selected by the collective focus group participants; however they are selected, there should be a common set across all the small groups answering the same question. The comparator institutions can be selected by the facilitator, large focus group or small discussion group; however, the comparators should include institutions with both a higher and lower quality or reputation in the area identified by the question. For example, if the focus group was answering a question about the factors that build a research reputation, the group would compare its own institution to one that has a higher and one that has a lower reputation. Comparing institutions which are both higher and lower provides information to estimate the level of weakness or strength of a given factor for the participant's institution.

Small groups start a strategy canvas by placing the selected factors on the x-axis of the strategy canvas. The group then evaluates and rates the comparator institutions on each of the factors, assigning a value ranging from low to high (with 1 as low and 5 as high, see Figure 3.2). This is followed by a discussion and rating of their own institution on each of the factors. The ratings are plotted on the y-axis of the strategy canvas, with the end result reflecting the differences across institutions in approaches to a given programme or set of activities. The canvas results can be used to generate further discussion on recommendations to be made to the institution's programme (or pillar) as part of their debrief to the larger focus group.

Figure 3.2 is an example of a strategy canvas structured to answer a question within the teaching pillar: "What factors will influence interest in professional graduate programmes in five years?" and reflects some of the discussions heard during the University of Calgary strategy sessions in 2011. Prior to completing this canvas participants should have read the environmental summary documents containing information on such trends

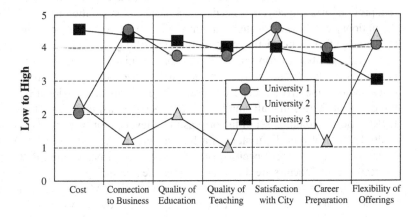

Figure 3.2 Strategy Canvas for Professional Graduate Programmes

as current and future enrolment patterns at their institution, current applicant backgrounds, practices in other graduate programmes, and employment of graduates. For the strategy grid in Figure 3.2 seven factors were identified based on the environmental summary documents and participant perceptions (x-axis in Figure 3.2).

University 1 is the participants' home university; while the two comparator universities are 2 and 3. University 2 has a lower reputation for its professional education programmes, with university 3 having a higher one. Each of the three institutions is rated from low to high on each factor (y-axis on Figure 3.2). After comparing their institution to the other two, participants discuss the differences across institutions and develop recommendations for changes to improve their university. The three recommendations from this group discussion were: the quality of the professional progammes does not need to be improved, as they are on par with the comparators; the tuition for professional graduate programmes is too low and should be increased as it is influencing perceptions of the quality of the programmes; and third, improving career preparation activities is an area that would distinguish the institution's programme from others.

The eliminate, reduce, raise, and create (ERRC) grid is also adapted, from Kim and Mauborgne's (2005, 2014) blue ocean discussion, to identify changes within a pillar or programme by reviewing internal factors. It differs from a strategy grid because it does not involve a comparison to external institutions. An ERRC grid provides a framework for groups to objectively discuss how different internal factors will contribute to the success of the institution's programmes in five to 10 years. The underlying assumption is that factors supporting current programmes and activities need to be adjusted in preparation for future disruptions, and these adjustments involve eliminating, reducing, or raising (enhancing) factors in existing programmes, or creating new ones.

As with the strategy canvas, the discussion is initiated by the facilitator posing a question to the large group such as, "What factors will increase research outcomes five years from now?" The facilitator then identifies three or four factors that all small break-out focus groups include on their ERRC grids. A common set of factors ensures a level of consistency across multiple small group discussions. Each small group can add one or two additional factors to their specific grid—this is the create part of the ERRC process—and all factors are then placed along the x-axis. Figure 3.3 shows an ERRC grid for the research outcomes question earlier (Blue Ocean Strategy, 2020). In this case, the first four factors were provided to all small groups: access to internal research funds as a bridge to external funding (i.e., bridge funds), support for interdisciplinary collaborations (i.e., collaboration), access to skilled researchers (i.e., research personnel), and support for increasing research findings beyond publications (i.e., translation). The last factor, administrative assistance in completing the necessary university processes (i.e., support), was identified in a small group discussion.

Each group first estimates the current status of each factor, using the five-point scale on the y-axis (from low to high). This step answers the question "Where are we now?" The score for each factor is generated through the small group's discussion and is placed on the grid as shown in the white bars on Figure 3.3. In this case, the group concluded that four of the factors were below acceptable levels (i.e., rated below 2.5). Although quantitative

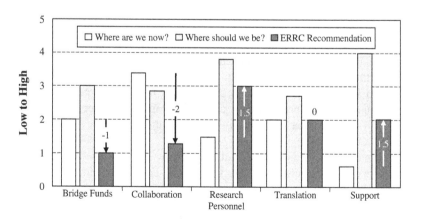

Figure 3.3 ERRC Grid for Building Research Capacity

measures are used, estimates are based on the small group members' experience and perceptions at the institution.

A second bar is then added to the grid by answering the question "Where should we be?" (middle bars in Figure 3.3). These estimates reflect how much a factor should be increased (or decreased) to reach an optimal outcome. For the example in Figure 3.3, the group decided that increases in four of the five factors would be needed. They concluded future research productivity would be increased if there was more internal bridge funding, additional post-doctoral scholars would increase the number of skilled researchers, improved access to expertise on commercialising research findings would diversify the research outcomes (translation), and more administrative support to deal with the processes needed to satisfy external funding agencies and internal requirements would reduce the time researchers had to spend on non-research activities.

The next step is for the group to review all the recommended changes (i.e., second bar for each factor) and decide which ones are the most critical. It is typical that the group will want all factors increased and avoid prioritising them. The goal of this step is to ensure that the final recommended changes (to the current levels) sum to zero; that is, the increase in some of the factors is counterbalanced by a decrease in other factors. This is the most important part of the group discussion. If the groups are not required to have their recommended changes across all the factors sum to zero, they avoid the difficult discussion as to the trade-offs that need to be made because of limited resources.

After discussing how to adjust each factor so the total change sums to zero, the new recommendations are placed on the grid as a third bar for each factor. These three steps of identifying the current level of a factor (bar one), optimal amount (bar 2), and prioritised amount (bar 3) guides the group through understanding the current situation, identifying the potential impact of a factor, and the trade-offs needed when resources are limited.

As shown in the figure, after discussing the acceptable trade-offs in the recommended changes, the small group's final ERRC recommendations were to increase research personnel and administrative support, and decrease support for interdisciplinary research (i.e., collaboration) and bridge funding. They felt that not increasing research personnel and administrative support would lead to future barriers in both effectiveness and efficiencies of research programmes. They were willing to accept a decrease in internal bridge funding and maintain the same level of support for commercialising research findings because these were not as strong barriers to producing high-quality research. They concluded that a decrease in support for interdisciplinary research would not influence collaborative research projects. If there was potential for a good collaborative project it would occur without additional support.

It is the not the actual scores on the ERRC Grid that are as important as the logic supporting the final recommendations. As in the case of the strategy canvas, once small groups complete their ERRC grid they summarise their discussion through three recommendations which are shared in the larger group debrief.

In summary, these two strategy exercises guide discussions towards identifying changes needed to improve programmes or activities, and prioritising these changes. Strategy canvases are good for groups of individuals who are aware of other university programmes and are sufficiently informed to make external comparisons. The ERRC grid is particularly relevant for individuals who are active in specific university programmes, and aware of their limitations and strengths. The completion of both the strategy canvas and ERRC grid should be based on perceptions, not exact measures. They are frameworks to guide discussions toward prioritising resources and programmes as well as identifying potential trade-offs. They are not intended to provide detailed changes in the current operations; rather, they should lead to a better understanding of existing strengths and weakness in institutional programmes, and where additional resources could lead to future opportunities.

Online Surveys

Online surveys are another form of high-impact engagement: they can lead to more detailed feedback from individual respondents compared to that collected in focus group discussions. They require fewer resources—financial and time—to gather feedback than through focus group discussions, and respondents can complete the survey when it fits their schedule. Online surveys can be conducted in parallel with the focus group sessions.

Other benefits of surveys are more individuals will complete a survey than participate in a focus group, responses are entered digitally, reducing the need for data input, and specific demographic data of the participants is more easily captured, leading to a better understanding of the issues associated with different constituencies. Surveys are more likely than focus group discussions to capture insightful ideas, since the dynamics of group discussions can lead to unique ideas falling through the cracks (Garvin & Roberto, 2001; Kahneman, Lovallo & Sibony, 2011).

Completing a survey does not require the same commitment as participating in a focus group, where individuals engage with others. In focus group discussions participants learn about issues or concerns in areas where they may have little experience; therefore, surveys are less effective at creating a shared view of the changes needed for a sustainable future.

Although surveys offer a lower resource-intensive alternative to focus groups, there is an upfront cost to their development. Well-framed questions are time-consuming to design, and surveys need to be structured so they can be completed in 20 minutes or less. If the strategic planning process includes both focus group discussions and a survey, the survey questions need to be aligned with those in the focus group.

As with focus group participants, survey respondents need to be encouraged to complete the background reading from the environmental summaries, and conclude with three recommendations for building a sustainable future. Their responses will also be based on perceptions and not exact measures. The survey data should be analysed for trends or common themes in the current programmes, and priorities for change or gaps in knowledge of the respondents.

The ERRC grid exercise discussed earlier can be adapted to a survey format by visually creating the grid through an existing survey programme. Separate grids and factors can be created for different questions within a pillar, and respondents can move bars up and down on the grid to reflect their views. In contrast, it is difficult to adapt a strategy canvas to the format of an online survey. One issue is comparing similar institutions on a given set of factors, since respondents vary in their knowledge of other organisations and cannot bridge these differences through conversations with other group members. As well, it is more difficult to have individuals visually create a strategy canvas with existing survey programmes. However, the questions used to guide the construction of a strategy canvas can be adapted into a survey format, and respondents can be asked to identify factors that they believe are influencing the outcomes of specific programmes in the university, and why or how they will influence future programmes.

Sharing Findings

One of the goals of the strategic planning process is to ensure that the institution's culture is effective and responsive to change, and achieving this goal requires communicating in a timely manner what was heard in the engagement exercises. The feedback should be aggregated into trends and patterns, and include both strategic (i.e., influencing the macro direction of the institution) and operational (i.e., influencing more micro activities) recommendations. Given the frontline experience of many of the participants, engagement exercises generate a significant amount of operational feedback, which is important to the future execution of the strategy. The feedback should include conflicting trends or patterns to build an understanding of the multiple viewpoints amongst stakeholders. Incorporation of this feedback into operational plan development and execution is discussed in Chapter 5.

A written report summarising the feedback should be broadly disseminated to stakeholders and accessible on the strategic planning process website. Dividing the summary feedback into separate reports—teaching, research, and community engagement—is helpful to stakeholders who are only interested in a particular pillar. To maintain the legitimacy of the process the information in these reports should include descriptions of the consultation activities, the methodologies used to analyse the data, demographic analyses of participants in relation to the university community, and perceptions of the current status of university programmes and recommended changes. These summary reports can present data with minimal interpretation, and include specific stories, from the focus group discussions, which are exemplars of real experiences by participants.

"Word clouds" provide a visualisation of the themes or trends identified in the engagement process (Boost Labs, 2014). Contents of a word cloud are the themes identified through an initial qualitative analysis of the feedback; the cloud provides a visual summary of the frequency of a particular theme. Sample comments need to accompany the word cloud to provide details on the type of feedback received as well as conflicting views held by stakeholders.

Figure 3.4 gives an example of a word cloud based on student focus groups exploring how their educational experience should shift over the next five years. Some of the concerns include the need for better integration of professional development and practical experiences for students (i.e., PD/practical/skills), a need to develop more consistent assessment methods of

Figure 3.4 Word Cloud for Teaching Pillar

student performance (i.e., varied/mixed assessment/evaluation), a need for more training for teaching assistants (i.e., TA/skills), concerns that students should have more access to English as a Second Language training (i.e., ESL), and increased recognition of student accomplishments (i.e., recognition). Although these particular themes would emerge on many campuses, a word cloud will reflect differing priorities depending on the dynamics of each university.

Summary

Stakeholder engagement is a critical step in supporting and enhancing a more effective institutional culture by integrating silos and reinforcing institutional responsiveness. The effectiveness of stakeholder engagement depends on informed participants and future-oriented discussions. It requires building an engagement platform for continuous communication during the engagement phase and ensuring access to a broad base of information so participants are all equally informed. Once formal engagement activities are completed, communication of the feedback in a timely manner supports transparency and an awareness of the multiple—and often conflicting—viewpoints held by stakeholders. Additional key points for informed engagement are listed in Table 3.8.

Table 3.8 Chapter Summary: Informed Engagement

- Strategy engagement is a two-way information exchange which is future-oriented. Structured stakeholder consultation creates opportunities to develop a broader perspective about the institution and its future, as well as providing forums for debate and input.
- An engagement platform, consisting of a communications strategy and environmental summaries, maximises stakeholder preparation and participation in the formal consultation process.
- A comprehensive communications strategy creates awareness and inspires stakeholders, while reinforcing consistent messages on the need for a strategic planning process and the value of individual contributions to future-proof the institution.
- Environmental summaries create a level playing field of knowledge. Access to information on external trends and opportunities, higher education best practices, and internal strengths and limitations allow participants to interpret and substantiate conclusions about current and desired future states.
- Meaningful consultation with stakeholders is part of a well-designed strategic planning process. The anticipated level of invested time and effort in specific stakeholder engagement activities should be in proportion to the feedback a specific group can provide.

(Continued)

Table 3.8 (Continued)

- Given the independent focus of academic faculty, in parallel with their expectations of being consulted on key decisions, it is particularly important that they have an opportunity to engage fully in the process so they are supportive once the final strategic goals are defined.
- High-impact engagement activities require upfront time and expertise to develop appropriate group tasks or survey questions, and formats for collecting and interpreting participant feedback. Focus group discussions and online surveys are two examples of high-impact consultation.
- The strategy canvas and ERRC grids are two engagement exercises that focus discussions and recommendations on the future of the university.
- Timely feedback to stakeholders on what was heard during consultation should include conflicting trends or patterns. This builds an understanding of the multiple viewpoints amongst stakeholders as to what the institution should be prioritising.
- A written report summarising the feedback should be broadly disseminated to stakeholders. Dividing the summary feedback into three separate reports— teaching, research, and community engagement—is helpful to stakeholders who may only have interest in a particular pillar.

---

4 Creating the Strategy

Strategy is a bridge between the institution's current and future states. This chapter outlines how this bridge aligns the university's multiple activities so that the knowledge it creates and disseminates are both relevant and valued by future stakeholders. A successful strategy guides the development of innovative and unique programmes valued by stakeholders.

According to business strategy guru Michael Porter (1985, 1996) a strategy should lead to one of three types of goals: becoming more focused, effective cost management, or serving unique markets. Each of these strategic goals leads to a different set of priorities and criteria for making decisions about the institution's future state. Examples of these strategic goals include eliminating or reducing programmes that are more effectively offered by other institutions (focus), modifying processes or practices to be the most cost-effective alternative (cost management), and building unique research programmes to attract funding from donors, government, or commercial organisations (differentiation). Although Porter (1996) concluded that businesses should focus on accomplishing one of these strategic goals, universities may need a strategy that leads to a combination of the three outcomes because of their broad mandates. For example, effective cost management might be critical in the ongoing delivery of non-academic services, increased focus may be needed to create more effective academic programmes, and differentiation may attract external funding for unique research programmes.

The processes leading to the identification and evaluation of strategic opportunities and the selection of strategic goals are described in this chapter. They are a series of filters that begin with the analysis and interpretation of three levels of information, leading to the identification of multiple opportunities, which are compared and evaluated to select a small number of goals that ensure a viable future. Once the strategic goals are identified, they need to be integrated into an overarching strategy statement that communicates where the institution is headed and how it will get there.

A strategy statement simplifies the complexity of the strategic plan so that it can be clearly communicated to stakeholders.

An effective strategy provides a unifying direction focused on the horizon, rather than detailed plans that outline step-by-step actions. However, the outcome of the strategic planning process is a framework for building an operational plan and budgets that drive the strategy into all levels of decision-making, which is discussed in Chapter 5. Table 4.1 highlights the two steps in Phase 3, which lead to a unifying strategy with a high level of awareness, while Figure 4.1 further details the components needed in each of the steps.

Table 4.1 Phase 3 of Five-Phase Strategic Planning Process

Phase 1: Setting the Stage	Phase 2: Informed Engagement	Phase 3: Creating the Strategy	Phase 4: Executing the Strategy	Phase 5: Future-Proofing
A. Dialoguing with stakeholders	A. Building an engagement platform	A. Developing the strategy	A. Converting strategy to operations	A. Communicating strategic impacts
B. Establishing legitimacy	B. Consulting with stakeholders	B. Building identity and awareness	B. Driving the operational plan	B. Enhancing an effective institutional culture

Figure 4.1 Components to Create the Strategy

Developing the Strategy

A strategy is formed through the integration of complex information, informed insight, and creativity (Porter, 1996). Given that the future is being predicted, choices and trade-offs are made with some degree of uncertainty. This uncertainty is mitigated through "sensemaking," which is developed by analysing multiple sources of information, understanding the institution's strengths and weaknesses, and reviewing external trends for the potential opportunities and threats they create (Gioia & Chittipeddi, 1991). Informed insight and creativity play an important role in identifying strategic opportunities, assessing their feasibility, and developing a coherent narrative to guide the institution towards its predicted future (Martin & Golsby-Smith, 2017; Sull et al., 2017).

Two key actions are needed to transition from consultation to strategy development (see Table 4.2). The first comprises the analysis and integration of three levels of data, and applying a SWOT (i.e., strengths, weaknesses, opportunities, and threats) framework to identify strategic opportunities that will lead to future sustainability (Learned et al., 1969). The second focuses on assessing these strategic opportunities through activity-systems maps and feasibility analysis to select the most appropriate strategic opportunities (Collis & Rukstad, 2008; Porter, 1996). The strategic plan is then finalised through a strategy statement and clear strategic goals, so that it is easily understood and creates the necessary platform for implementation which is covered in Chapter 5.

Identifying Strategic Opportunities

Building an appropriate institutional strategy requires the analysis and integration of three levels of data. Figure 4.2 illustrates the integration of these levels of data into a SWOT framework which, through informed insight and sensemaking, leads to the identification of strategic opportunities for assessment and evaluation.

Table 4.2 Developing the Strategy

Actions	Outcome
• Identification of strategic opportunities through multi-level data integration and SWOT analysis • Assessment of strategic opportunities using activity-systems maps and feasibility analysis, and development of a strategy document with unifying strategy statement and goals	Clear strategy to future-proof the institution

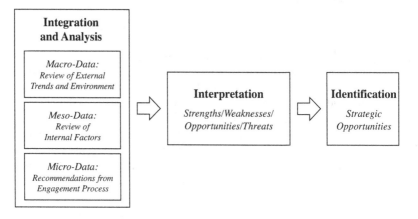

Figure 4.2 Process to Identify Strategic Opportunities

Micro-level data is derived from the recommendations collected from focus group discussions and survey responses. These recommendations are analysed through qualitative analysis tools to identify dominant themes, which reflect factors influencing the effectiveness of activities within the teaching, research, and community engagement pillars. They provide information about the impact, or perceived value, of current programmes, plans, and processes. Many of the ideas emerging from this analysis have an operational focus; however, given that faculty and staff have front-line interactions with other stakeholders they often sense early signals of changing expectations and needs, such as satisfaction or dissatisfaction with a programme or initiative.

Data at the meso-level includes institutional-level factors and processes that are significantly influenced or controlled by the president and other senior leaders. This information will have been summarised in the documents created for the engagement processes (see Chapter 3, Table 3.4). These factors include allocation of financial resources, investments in physical and technical infrastructure (e.g., buildings, laboratories, equipment, information technology), and support services or programmes (e.g., financial administration, human resources, marketing, alumni). Understanding the impact of these factors on the activities in each pillar is critical because they are the levers that can be used to initiate and implement change.

Factors at the macro level may have the most influence over the institution's future, yet leaders have the least control over them. They include external technological, demographic, and sociological trends, government regulations and funding principles, and the structure of the local and national economies, all of which are consolidated using the PESTLE analysis as discussed in Chapter 3.

These three levels of data need to be integrated and interpreted, and a common framework for this step is a SWOT analysis. A SWOT is a user-friendly way of interpreting the internal processes as strengths and weakness, and the trends in the external environment as opportunities or threats. Determining which factors or findings are strengths or weaknesses is accomplished through comparisons to other institutions, particularly those with identified best practices. Similarly, determining which factors or findings are threats or opportunities is assessed in terms of the institution's ability to respond. Once complete, the SWOT analysis provides a framework for identifying strategic opportunities and a rationale for why an institution needs to respond to certain threats.

Table 4.3 provides an example of a SWOT analysis, where each of the listed strengths, weaknesses, opportunities, and threats were identified through the analysis of the three levels of information. An institution's combination of strengths leads to capabilities that support effective delivery of programmes or activities within a pillar. Existing weaknesses, insufficient research funding as an example, can limit the development of capabilities and needed changes. Some of the identified threats will impact many institutions, such as increased competition for students, while some of the opportunities will be unique to an institution because of its combination of strengths and weaknesses, and operating context.

The results of a SWOT analysis should be further refined by answering the questions in Table 4.4, which guide the analysis towards selecting feasible alternatives.

Table 4.3 SWOT Analysis Example

Strengths	Weaknesses
• Highly rated research teams in select areas • Growing student demand • Innovative academic programmes • Relatively new infrastructure • Engaged and supportive community	• Insufficient research funding • Inefficiencies in operating systems • Negative student feedback on overall educational experience • Lagging reputational rankings
Opportunities	*Threats*
• High employment rates • Burgeoning start-up ecosystem • Growing 18-25 age cohort • Generous philanthropic community	• Reduced government funding • New educational institutions competing for students • Emerging technology disruptions • Increasing wage demands

Table 4.4 Questions to Identify Strategic Opportunities

• What are the most significant consequences of current trends?
• How will these trends influence stakeholder expectations/needs?
• Do some programmes/activities need to be reduced to sustain other ones?
• Is there capacity to build new specialised programmes and set new directions?
• What internal barriers could limit needed changes?
• What threats or risks must be reduced in order to satisfy future needs?

Some of the identified strategic opportunities will be for generic programmes (i.e., those offered by most universities) and parallel strategic choices for businesses competing in the "red ocean." A red ocean is defined as a market segment where competition is based on offering a better product for a lower price within a relatively fixed market space (Kim & Mauborgne, 2005). Red oceans in higher education occur where institutions compete for students in commonly offered educational programmes or for funds in conventional research activities. In these generic programmes, the discussion needs to focus on predicting the impact of external trends, and identifying changes needed to ensure these programmes are still valued by stakeholders in the future. This may lead to an increased focus on certain programmes while dropping less sustainable ones, or enhancing effectiveness through the use of new technologies. These are difficult decisions, but it is these trade-offs that are the basis of an effective strategy (Collis & Rukstad, 2008).

The more creative part of strategic planning is identifying strategic opportunities, or sweet spots, that are unique alternatives, align with the organisation's capabilities, and satisfy future stakeholder interests (Collis & Rukstad, 2008). These sweet spots are also known as "blue oceans" in business strategies (Kim & Mauborgne, 2005). A blue ocean is a market segment where there is potential for high growth because the company has used its capabilities to develop a unique product which serves specific needs. Higher education institutions can create blue oceans by responding to emerging research or educational opportunities through the development of internal strengths and capabilities, and distinctive programmes. These new programmes may be based on needs within the institution's specific context (e.g., regional economy), or a much broader set of goals (e.g., national) (Porter, 1996; Kim & Mauborgne, 2005).

Developing blue ocean programmes generally requires more resources than building capacity in red ocean spaces; however, if they are successful they will have a greater influence on an institution's reputation, as they more clearly differentiate an institution from its peers. The justification for developing a unique new programme or sweet spot needs to be understood and endorsed by a broad range of stakeholders because of the costs and risks involved. The justification should answer the questions "Why?" and "Where?"; while the "How?" needs to be addressed by the operational plan, which is discussed in Chapter 5. As suggested by Eckel and Trower (2019), "Think compass, not map."

Once both red and blue ocean opportunities have been identified they need to be evaluated in terms of the institution's capacity, resource requirements, feasibility of success, and institutional ambition. Having an overly ambitious strategic plan that cannot be reasonably implemented does not serve an institution or its stakeholders. A mapping process to evaluate various strategic opportunities and select the best ones is discussed next.

Mapping to Strategy

The identified strategic opportunities need to be prioritised in terms of institutional capacity and capabilities to support new initiatives, and the resources required to elevate current outcomes. The comparison of opportunities may require an iterative process to identify the most feasible and have the greatest impact on the institution's future.

One tool to assess strategic opportunities is an activity-systems map (Porter, 1996; Collis & Rukstad, 2008). This map links strategic opportunities to the supporting programmes or activities required to achieve success. It also illustrates how different combinations of activities interact to support a strategic opportunity, and can be used to determine existing limitations or barriers which need to be addressed. Figure 4.3 shows an activity-systems map for the teaching pillar based on the University of Calgary's "Eyes High" strategy (see Appendix) (University of Calgary, 2011). It consists of five strategic goals that are in the second lightly shaded circle in the figure. They include improving the quality of instruction, formally measuring the outcomes of academic programmes, building research skills, increasing the breadth of student experiences, and increasing the flexibility of learning opportunities.

The programmes and activities supporting the five strategic goals are in the third concentric circle in Figure 4.3. For example, high quality instruction requires increased opportunities for the professional development of teaching, as well as for research-informed teaching and learning practices (often referred to as the scholarship of teaching and learning—SOTL). Formally measured outcomes require assessment of academic programmes through regular and comprehensive reviews with accountabilities for continuous improvement, as well as defined learning outcomes for each programme. Each strategic goal is analysed and represented accordingly, and as reflected

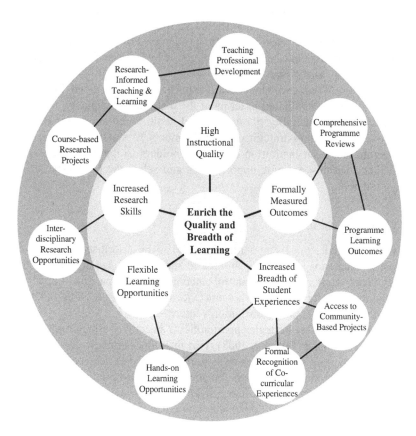

Figure 4.3 Activity-Systems Map for Undergraduate Teaching and Learning Strategic Goals

in the figure, the activity-systems map also shows the cross-linkages between the different activities since many are inter-dependent or synergistic.

Once the requirements for developing a strategic opportunity are understood, the level of needed change to bridge the existing and desired future states can be assessed and, in turn, the feasibility of successfully developing the opportunity. A feasibility analysis for two of the goals in the activity-systems map earlier is shown in Table 4.5. Each strategic goal is accompanied by its supporting programme and activities, and the assessment of the current and desired states is based on the analysis of the engagement data and environmental summaries. The level of required change and/or investment required to bridge from the current to the desired state is categorised as high, medium, or low.

Table 4.5 Strategic Opportunity Feasibility Analysis for Two Strategic Goals

Strategic Goal	Supporting Programme or Activity	Current State	Desired State	Required Change and/or Investment (H, M, L)*
High-Quality Instruction	Teaching Professional Development	• Limited professional development opportunities and lack of visibility on campus	• Professional development of teaching to create a culture of expert instruction	M
	Research-informed Teaching and Learning	• Siloed research on teaching and learning, and application to practice	• Teaching excellence through integration of research	H
Formally Measured Outcomes	Comprehensive Programme Reviews	• Basic programme reviews at inconsistent intervals	• Comprehensive programme reviews to identify programme learning outcomes	M
	Programme Learning Outcomes	• Inconsistent development and use of programme learning outcomes	• Programmes guided by measurable outcomes	H

* H = high level of change and/or investment required to meet desired future state; M = medium level of change and/or investment required; L = low level of change/investment needed

Table 4.5 shows that there is some capacity and programming in each of the strategic goal areas, but further work needs to be done to reach the desired state. In the case of the "high-quality instruction" strategic goal, considerable change and investment is needed to deliver on "teaching excellence through integration of research," since the current work is siloed across campus and not broadly applied to practice. A centralised hub to support various disciplines through innovative pedagogy development and technology integration would be required to meet this goal.

Similarly, for the "formally measured outcomes" goal, the current state shows a level of inconsistency in the development and use of programme learning outcomes, compared to the desired state where all programmes would be guided by measurable outcomes. It is expected this goal will require significant change management initiatives, since many faculty members and academic units will resist such an initiative.

There are no specific guidelines for determining the feasibility of a strategic opportunity, since it depends on the overall ambition of the institution and its stakeholders, as well as the potential for increased investment to support growth and development. As an example, if the programmes and initiatives in every strategic goal require a high level of change and investment, the strategic opportunity may be overly ambitious. If this is deemed to be the case, a decision needs to be made to adjust or modify accordingly. This can be done as part of a creative thinking approach, which is stimulated by developing different activity-systems maps, particularly if they are completed for contrasting, or different combinations of, strategic goals (Collis & Rukstad, 2008). Comparing different activity-systems maps may lead to additional insight regarding the resources required to support different programmes and the feasibility of combining internal strengths to create the necessary capabilities for achieving strategic goals. The final result is a defined number of strategic opportunities—each with a limited number of strategic goals—which are aligned with each of the pillars of teaching, research, and community engagement, and which are deemed to balance ambition and feasibility.

Table 4.6 gives an example of the final strategic opportunities incorporated into the University of Calgary's Eyes High strategy (see Appendix). Alternative strategic opportunities were also developed from the data integration and SWOT process described earlier in this chapter but were rejected through the evaluation and feasibility process as described in the following section.

After the final strategic opportunities and goals are selected through iteration and refinement, the next step is to construct the strategy document

Table 4.6 Example of Strategic Opportunities

Strategic Opportunity	Pillars Impacted
• Align the university with the global and enterprising values of the City of Calgary	• Teaching, Research, and Community Engagement
• Enrich and enhance the learning environment through immersion in research and hands-on experiences	• Teaching and Research
• Incorporate entrepreneurial thinking into the culture of the university	• Teaching, Research, and Community Engagement
• Elevate research excellence on international standards in select focus areas of strength	• Research

that will guide the institution towards the goals. Key components of this document are an overarching strategy statement, the strategic goals for each pillar (including—at a high level—what needs to be done to achieve the goals), and other supporting information on the engagement process and institutional values.

All of the analysis from the variety of sources considered in the strategic planning process should culminate in the development of the strategy statement. A strategy statement is a short—35 words or less—summary of the institution's future direction (Collis & Rukstad, 2008); in it, the complexity of strategic planning is reduced to elegant simplicity. Its wording is critical, since it will be the flagbearer, representing the strategy as a whole; it is often the most visible aspect of a strategic plan. The statement's narrative needs to be crisp, inspirational and accessible by a broad range of stakeholders. It should contain a concise description of the value the institution will create in the next five years (i.e., why stakeholders should support the institution) and the breadth of strategic goals to be achieved (i.e., scope). Its brevity encourages reading, and its clarity leads to understanding, and therefore acceptance, of the strategy (Collis & Rukstad, 2008).

As an example, the strategy statement developed during the University of Calgary's strategic planning process in 2016–17, is as follows:

> The University of Calgary is a global intellectual hub located in Canada's most enterprising city. In this spirited, high-quality learning environment, students will thrive in programs made rich by research, hands-on experiences and entrepreneurial thinking. By 2022, we will be recognized as one of Canada's top five research universities, fully engaging the communities we both serve and lead.
>
> (University of Calgary, 2017:p.3)

This statement provided a concise description of the value that the university intended to create for its primary communities, the range of opportunities that it would support (scope), and the strategic goal of being a top-five research university (measurable target) over the next five years. It also explicitly stated a vision for the university: to become a leading research institution as benchmarked against peers, to enhance the learning environment with and through research, and to become an intellectual hub engaging the community in learning and research activities. The supporting strategic goals were aligned to three foundational commitments in teaching, research, and community engagement. Further information on the strategy and its implementation can be found in the Appendix.

Once the strategic plan has been created with the inclusion of the strategy statement and goals, the oversight committee needs to present it to various stakeholder groups for discussion and refinement prior to the formal approval process. The academic senate and board, and the vice-presidents and deans are essential participants at this stage since, as ambassadors of the plan, they will need to be knowledgeable and require awareness to support the preparation of campus for the upcoming changes. Discussions should focus around refining different points rather than changing the logic or the goals. The final strategic plan should then be approved by the academic senate and board, where there should be strong support for the strategy and its goals.

Building Identity and Awareness

An approved strategic plan is a significant milestone: it offers clarity about the goals needed to move the institution forward. The resulting document encapsulates both months of work under the leadership of the strategic oversight and working committees, and a process, which engaged a significant number of stakeholders across and beyond the campus. It contains an exciting vision for the future, which needs to be communicated. The support of the larger body of stakeholders needs to be reinvigorated, as it has likely been several months since they were directly involved in the planning process.

In order to build support and awareness, a communications plan is needed. The plan should be structured to reach and engage internal and external stakeholders through multiple communication channels. Two components of the communications plan—the identity and launch of the strategic plan document—are discussed in this section. Additional elements of a communications plan include webpages, targeted advertising, and social media campaigns. The overall communications plan should be led by the marketing and communications team, augmented by external expertise as needed.

The identity of the strategic plan needs to reinforce the institutional brand. This starts with the title, which is a critical decision since it influences subsequent communications throughout the tenure of the strategic plan. The title needs to resonate with stakeholders, be remembered—and referred to—as part of the institution's vernacular, and should reinforce the line-of-sight concept by linking the strategy to action.

The style and tone of the communications, particularly during the launch to the community, influences the longevity of awareness of the strategy and acceptance of its implementation. The result should be a strategy that is both recognizable and broadly supported. These actions are listed in Table 4.7 and are discussed further in this chapter.

Table 4.7 Building Identity and Awareness

Actions	Outcome
• Development of a unique identity for the strategy which reinforces the institution's brand • Communication plan development to publicly launch the strategy to create awareness and signal implementation	Strategy that is recognizable and broadly supported

Reinforcing the Brand

Organisational branding was first developed in the corporate sector to create and promote an identity and multiple touchpoints to build coherence between strategy, organisational culture, and stakeholder perception. An effective brand aligns the organisation's vision, culture, and image (Balmer & Greyser, 2003).

Every higher education institution inherently has a brand: it is the combination of intangible assets like longstanding traditions, geographic location, well-known alumni, internationally recognised faculty, research impacts, student experiences, and the emotional connection between it and its stakeholders. These factors combine to form a unique presence, or brand, which can be used to create a marketable image. Many institutions have a brand that has been intentionally created or explicitly articulated, and is nurtured to improve their reputation through various activities and initiatives (Mampaey & Huisman, 2016).

The brand of an academic institution is important to both its external and internal stakeholders. A positive brand aids in both the recruitment of high-quality faculty and students, and the attraction of significant philanthropic funding. Promoting the brand internally encourages faculty, staff, and students to deepen their attachment to the organisation and its value (Clark, Chapleo & Suomi, 2019). This can impact their interest in transforming the organisation through making the brand value a reality, which in turn can enhance the overall effectiveness of the institution's culture.

Brand development and management are growing in importance as the higher education marketplace becomes increasingly competitive. It is thus strategically important to create images that match the organisational identity of an institution, and transmit an institution's brand in a concrete way (Stensaker, 2007).

The development of a new strategic plan is an opportunity to reinforce an institution's existing brand or to begin to shape a new one. The content of the strategy document should be the critical foundation to do this; however, the presentation of the plan through the look and feel of the public document influences both internal and external stakeholder perceptions as

Table 4.8 Key Considerations for Strategic Plan Identity Elements

Strategic Plan Element	Key Considerations
Title	• Will the title be used and remembered in the vernacular of the institution by stakeholders?
Introduction and framing	• Does the introduction to the strategy, as well as the language that wraps around the content, inspire the reader?
Imagery	• Are the photos reinforcing the message in terms of the diversity and type of stakeholder groups represented, being action-oriented, and capturing key campus locations or iconography?
Colours and graphics	• Do the colours, graphics, and text size used for the strategy energise stakeholders?
Tactility	• Physical document: Does the size, shape, and type of paper invite the reader to open the document and turn the pages?

to the relevance and value of the strategy. These initial perceptions have long-term implications for the implementation and acceptance of the strategy. Creating a compelling identity for the strategy goes beyond its initial launch as awareness of the strategy's role in decision-making needs to be reinforced at multiple stages as discussed in Chapters 5 and 6. Experts from the marketing and communications professions are best suited to lead this work since they can accurately capture the tone and tenor of the strategic plan to maximum impact in the broader community. The president should establish a small committee made up of a few institutional leaders and stakeholders to work with this team and external consultants in managing the process.

Many elements go into a physical (or virtual) document to motivate a reader to open and digest it. Table 4.8 summarises some the key considerations when translating the strategic plan to a final format for release to stakeholders. The overall objective is to ensure that the strategy's identity is compelling and can be used to reinforce or shape the institutional brand.

Launching to the Community

Building or reinforcing a brand through the public document requires stakeholder awareness of the strategy and that it will be used to drive future decisions and investments. Awareness starts with an appropriate launch of the strategy by convening stakeholders to celebrate the closing of the planning process, thanking them for their contributions in shaping the final strategy, and signaling the start of implementation.

The benefits of a formal launch event include: (1) the ability to mark an important milestone in the institution's history by recognizing the start of a new era, (2) an opportunity for the president to publicly commit to delivering on the vision and goals of the strategy, (3) reassurance to stakeholders that there is collective ownership of the strategy, and (4) a celebration of an exciting future, which will drive the commitment of stakeholders to align and support the strategy.

The format of the launch event should respect institutional culture and practices while signalling that there is something new on the horizon. Multiple supporting events may be held, including those targeted towards faculty, staff and students, and others for alumni or donors. Launch events should also be supported by other mechanisms to communicate the new strategy including a website, social media, and media coverage, as examples.

Summary

Three critical factors influencing the success of an institutional strategy are informed insight, the development of a narrative that provides the logic for the strategic choices made, and buy-in by stakeholders. Although a strategy needs to be based on a formal analysis of the different factors influencing the viability of the institution, it is still directed towards the future, which is anything but certain. A successful strategy is based on rigorous analysis and integration of data, identifying different alternatives, and selecting the most viable strategic opportunities to support the ambition of the institution. Supportive stakeholders are willing participants in strategy implementation.

Table 4.9 summarises the key points in the chapter.

Table 4.9 Chapter Summary: Creating the Strategy

- An important outcome of a strategic planning process is a clear narrative with supporting goals that reduces the complexity of the multiple forms of information gathered, and is a unifying vision towards the university's future.
- Strategic opportunities are identified by analyzing and integrating various levels of data. A SWOT analysis assists in the interpretation of the data. The identified opportunities should be at a high enough level that they do not deviate towards the granular level of an operational plan.
- Strategic opportunities should include "sweet spots" which occur in "blue oceans." These are unique directions that satisfy future needs within the institution's specific context (e.g., regional economy), or a much broader set of stakeholders (e.g., national).
- Identified strategic opportunities are assessed to determine which ones best balance the ambition of the institution and its stakeholders with expected capacity and resources. A useful tool to assess strategic opportunities is an activity-systems map.

(Continued)

Table 4.9 (Continued)

- The final strategy document is based on the selected strategic opportunities and its key components are an overarching strategy statement, the strategic goals for each pillar, and other supporting information on the engagement process and institutional values.
- A strategy statement is a short, 35 words or less, summary of the institution's future direction and is often the most visible aspect of a strategic plan. It is crisp, inspirational, and accessible by a broad range of stakeholders.
- Once the strategic plan is created, it is presented to various stakeholder groups for discussion and refinement prior to the formal approval process. Discussions focus around refining different points rather than changing the logic or the goals.
- A comprehensive communications plan is developed for the strategic plan, which engages internal and external stakeholders through multiple channels. Development of this plan is led by the marketing and communications team, augmented by external expertise as needed.
- The identity of the strategic plan reinforces the institutional brand. The title of the strategic plan needs to resonate with stakeholders, and become part of the institution's vernacular. The "look and feel" of the public document influences both internal and external stakeholder perceptions as to the relevance and value of the strategy.
- As part of a comprehensive communications plan, the strategic plan should be formally launched by convening stakeholders to highlight the strategic plan's goals and thank them for their contributions, create awareness of the strategy, and signal the start of implementation.

---

5   Executing the Strategy

In previous chapters, the focus is on the creation of a strategic plan that is future-oriented—one that is informed by environmental trends, shaped by best practice, and molded by stakeholder input and aspirations. A strategy positions an institution at a new starting line—one that is clear in terms of a desired future state. The success of the strategy, however, is in its disciplined execution, and the resulting impact on its stakeholders and community.

A strategy with a clear vision provides a framework to align the diverse academic and support units of an institution. It also signals to external stakeholders where their support and contributions will facilitate the building of the institution's future. However, a strategy is only window dressing if it does not guide operational decisions; all the work put into identifying trends and building a culture of engagement is wasted if the strategy does not become part of the institution's "DNA." This requires specific steps which are discussed in this chapter, along with consistent communication and a strong institutional culture which are discussed in Chapter 6. All combined, this creates a "movement" in the institution and the broader community towards the strategic goals.

The institutional strategic plan serves as a guide for broader planning and decision-making processes. The work of academic and non-academic units, allocation of resources, communication efforts, fundraising objectives, and government relations activities should all be aligned with the strategy. It provides a common platform to maintain consistency across the organisation, and to drive coherent messaging externally, which is important when engaging in activities such as fundraising and government advocacy.

The successful translation of a strategy into tangible results and outcomes takes committed and sustained effort; when a strategy never moves past the president's desk, or becomes merely a public relations exercise, the status quo is reinforced. Most university strategic plans only identify outcomes and do not include the priorities or metrics needed to guide decision-making for the execution of the plan, and thus fail to be implemented (Eckel & Trower, 2019).

The saying "vision without execution is hallucination," often attributed to Thomas Edison, is unfortunately true. When the strategy is launched with great fanfare, but without follow-through, it shortly disappears from conversations on and off campus. The most difficult part of strategy development is its implementation, since that is when the clear, and often tough, decisions need to be made (Pritchard, 2018).

It is the responsibility of the president to ensure that the strategy is integrated into all levels of decision-making. This is best accomplished through a clear operational plan, ongoing communication, and monitoring of progress towards strategic goals. Translation of strategy into action involves many people and it is crucial that, starting with the executive leadership team, there is ownership and accountability to execute the strategy across the institution.

Figure 5.1 illustrates the various steps that translate strategy into action and impact. Starting on the left, the strategic plan sets out goals and answers the question "Where do we want to go?" To answer the question "How will we get there?" an operational plan is developed—through broad consultation and leadership by the executive team—to provide a roadmap from the current state to the desired state. The roadmap begins with a five-year operational plan to inform annual business plans and budgets, followed by performance and work plans to align the efforts of the campus leaders and the governing bodies. The activity-systems maps, discussed in Chapter 4, become a key planning tool in developing the roadmap. The operational plan lays out the pathway for the different activity-systems in the institution (see Chapter 4). It provides further details on resource trade-offs, specific activities that need to be developed, and Key Performance Indicators (KPIs) for the tenure of the strategic plan.

Once the strategic and operational plans are in place, activities need to be phased to manage workflow. This can be a challenge, since institutional leaders will want to show progress by delivering some quick wins. Thus, the

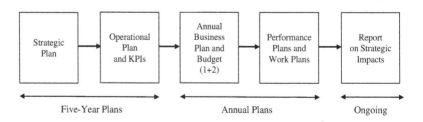

Figure 5.1 Translating Strategy into Action and Impact

president needs to ensure that the pace of execution aligns with the strategy and the operational plan over the five-year period. Managing the pace of the executive leadership team is particularly important, since the operationalisation of the strategic plan becomes their primary responsibility. This can be done through annual business plans that are linked to both the strategic goals and operational plan. The business plan should have a one-year time horizon with projected plans and budgets for the following two years (a 1+2 approach), such that a strategic plan guides five annual business plans.

A key responsibility of the president is to monitor the business plan so that it is based on the priorities in the operational plan. The budget also needs to lead to the development of, or reduction in, activities needed to achieve the strategic goals. It is critical for the president, in collaboration with the executive team, to ensure decision-making is continuously in alignment with the strategy. This involves following a well-defined and transparent process to develop a business plan that attracts the necessary resources and invests in activities that support progress towards the strategic goals. The business plan informs the performance plans for the president and the executive team, as well as the work to be done by the board and the academic senate. All of these activities ultimately support the strategy. The development of performance and work plans is discussed in a following section.

The final steps in translating the strategy into action are measuring and communicating impact. As shown in Figure 5.1, these are ongoing activities, since communication efforts need to be sustained. This is discussed in detail in Chapter 6.

When the processes in Figure 5.1 are followed there is a line-of-sight between the strategy and its intended outcomes, including visibility between the strategic goals and the pathway to achieving them, the pace at which the work should progress, the responsibilities of key individuals and bodies, and

Table 5.1 Phase 4 of Five-Phase Strategic Planning Process

Phase 1: Setting the Stage	Phase 2: Informed Engagement	Phase 3: Creating the Strategy	Phase 4: Executing the Strategy	Phase 5: Future-Proofing
A. Dialoguing with stakeholders	A. Building an engagement platform	A. Developing the strategy	A. Converting strategy to operations	A. Communicating strategic impacts
B. Establishing legitimacy	B. Consulting with stakeholders	B. Building identity and awareness	B. Driving the operational plan	B. Enhancing an effective institutional culture

Figure 5.2 Components to Support Strategy Execution

clarity on progress. This clarity makes it straightforward for the president to convey to the internal and external communities how the strategy is being delivered.

The following sections discuss these concepts in further detail, from bridging strategy and operations through the creation of an operational plan and the selection of KPIs. Implementation of the operational plan through the development of an annual business plan and linkage to leadership performance frameworks are also discussed. These steps are shaded in Table 5.1 with specific components illustrated in Figure 5.2.

Converting Strategy to Operations

During the strategic planning process, the consultation discussions should focus on the future, as opposed to reviewing operational issues. Prior to the 1990s the conventional logic was that developing strategy involved detailed planning, including budgets and internal processes. One of the most cited business scholars, Henry Mintzberg (1994, 1996), shifted this thinking by arguing that strategy creation and operational planning are different processes and should be conducted by different groups within an organisation.

Table 5.2 illustrates the differences between strategic and operational thinking. The goal of strategic thinking, hence strategic planning, is to predict where the organisation should be in the future based on environmental scanning and, more importantly, informed insight and creativity (Gavetti, 2012; Kaplan & Norton, 2005; Wang, 2010). In contrast, operational

Table 5.2 Strategic versus Operational Thinking

Strategic Thinking: Making Predictions	Operational Thinking: Achieving Outcomes
• Question assumptions • Identify risks • Set direction and goals • Choose what not to do	• Select priorities • Develop budgets to support priorities • Develop processes to mitigate risks • Measure outcomes and impacts

Table 5.3 Bridging Strategy and Operations

Actions	Outcome
• Development of priorities, objectives, and timelines to ensure strategic goals are achieved • Selection of KPIs to measure and benchmark progress	Roadmap to operationalise the strategy

thinking and planning focus on achieving shorter term outcomes that prepare an organisation for the predicted future.

The differences between strategic and operational thinking illustrate why an operational plan should not be developed until the strategy has been finalised. Separating strategy ("where") and operations ("how") simplifies the process: the strategic plan is about having a unified direction, and forms the framework for making difficult decisions about what priorities to develop, adjust, or eliminate during operational planning.

Table 5.3 lists the actions to build a roadmap that integrates the strategy into decisions. The first action is to develop priorities, objectives and timelines that will ensure the organisation meets its strategic goals. The second action is to identify KPIs that will measure and benchmark progress towards the strategic goals. An additional outcome of a clear strategy and operational plan is that they support enterprise risk management (ERM), which is an important component of higher education institutional management and oversight (Mattie, 2007).

Developing the Operational Plan

An institutional strategy will fail if it is not linked to the operational plan because, without this linkage, it is difficult to build accountabilities within the executive team and communicate progress to stakeholders. The operational plan should be easily understood and widely circulated, since many stakeholders will use it to understand how their activities link to, and are influenced by, the strategic plan.

The process to develop the operational plan should be similar to the one used for strategy development. It may be abbreviated, but will likely still require a number of months of effort. A consultative model grounded in inclusivity is essential, since the operational plan is where the "rubber hits the road," and stakeholders have a significant interest in its outcome. Planners should focus on the operational processes and barriers that were identified in the engagement feedback discussed in Chapters 3 and 4. Additional feedback gathered to augment this information should be operational rather than strategic, and provide specific details on barriers limiting the effective use of human, capital, and financial resources, and the identification of priorities, processes, and programmes that should be eliminated, modified, or developed.

There are different costs and benefits associated with creating one or multiple operational plans. An operational plan that covers all of the units within an institution may lead to better coordination across units, but be too long and complicated for use by diverse stakeholders. An alternative model is to separate the academic and research plans so there are two stand-alone plans, which are linked but can be used separately. While this approach may lead to a clearer understanding of priorities within each pillar, a risk is that it may reinforce traditional silos. The activities in the community engagement pillar can be integrated into each of these two plans when their activity-systems maps overlap, or a separate operational plan can be developed independently for this pillar.

Development of the operational plan(s) should rely on information from three main sources. The first is a literature review on trends in higher education, which may be an expansion of the environmental summaries completed for the strategic planning process (see Chapter 3). Additional information and benchmarking on specific targets and programmes, such as diversity, sustainability, or even facilities development, may need to be included.

A second source of information is the consultation feedback. As mentioned in Chapter 3, many of the recommendations and comments from the focus groups and online surveys will relate to operational details because participants are most familiar with operational issues and are rarely expected to think about strategic issues in their daily work.

Finally, the executive leadership team may choose to do further consultation, specific to operational planning, with relevant stakeholders. This consultation would gather additional information directly from decision-makers who will be implementing the operational plan. Its focus would be to identify potential barriers or strengths that will influence implementation of the strategic plan (e.g., emerging research strengths, status of research facilities, quality of classrooms, availability of teaching capacity for new programmes). This information may be collected through surveys, face-to-face

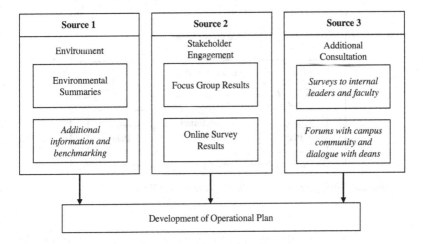

Source 1	Source 2	Source 3
Environment	Stakeholder Engagement	Additional Consultation
Environmental Summaries	Focus Group Results	*Surveys to internal leaders and faculty*
Additional information and benchmarking	Online Survey Results	*Forums with campus community and dialogue with deans*

Development of Operational Plan

Figure 5.3 Sources of Input to Develop the Operational Plan

forums, town halls, and one-on-one meetings with relevant unit leaders. Figure 5.3 lists these various sources with italicised text representing new sources to be consulted.

Responsibility for the development of the operational plans—assuming they are split between academic and research—should be with the provost and vice president (academic) (PVPA) and the vice president (research) (VPR) since they are ultimately accountable for teaching and learning, and research and scholarship outcomes. These two individuals need to work as a team so that academic and research priorities are not in silos but are synergistic. The president's responsibilities are twofold: to ensure that the operational plans support the overall institutional strategy, and to make certain there are no conflicts in priority setting or resource allocation between operational plans. Other executive team members support these plans through their portfolios.

Components of an operational plan include strategic priorities, objectives, timelines, and KPIs. The number of priorities in the operational plan should be limited to three to five for ease of understanding and communication. However, there also needs to be sufficient detail to permit decisions and specify deliverables relating to human, capital, and financial resource allocation which are itemised in the ensuing business plans. This detail is achieved through the inclusion of sub-priorities and objectives. The structure of the operational plan should lead to the identification of performance measures that can be summarised in dashboards or scorecards to report on

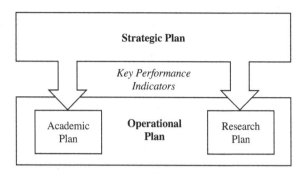

Figure 5.4 Linkage of Strategic Plan to Operational Plan

progress, which are discussed in Chapter 6. Leaders at all levels must be invested in this process to ensure priorities are aligned with the strategy and broadly communicated.

Once the operational plan has been developed through a consultative and iterative process with stakeholders, it needs approval through the appropriate governance body, which is normally the academic senate. It should be presented to the board for information, and possibly formal approval, depending on the institution's governance structure. Once approved, the operational plan should be formally launched to the internal community. This event should celebrate and thank stakeholders for their efforts in shaping the plan and confirm the operational plan to support the strategy is complete and being initiated. In addition, the work of the board and the academic senate should be tied to the strategy and operational plan in a transparent manner.

Figure 5.4 shows the relationship between the strategic and operational plans, and the KPIs which are used to monitor the strategy's impact.

Selecting Key Performance Indicators

Once a strategic plan has been launched, stakeholder commitment and its perceived legitimacy are influenced by the level of visible progress towards the stated goals. Evaluating and reporting tangible progress requires a set of performance metrics linked to specific outcomes. Common phrases used in organisational planning, such as "what gets measured gets managed" and "what gets managed gets done," emphasise the importance of having KPIs to assess the strategy's impact through metrics for evaluation, monitoring progress, and benchmarking. They also provide accountability for the president and other institutional leaders, and a means for the board to evaluate the effectiveness of the strategic plan and the president's performance.

Within the higher education sector, assessment of university performance using metrics occurs at three levels. At a macro level, governments (or other agencies) evaluate the performance of an identified group of universities in relation to those in another region or country (e.g., Weingarten et al., 2015). The next level of assessments involve performance based-funding (PBF) where governments review the performance of the universities to which they are contributing funds through prescribed and institutionally selected metrics (Usher, 2019b). These performance measures allow the government to evaluate an institution over time, and within a jurisdiction, with the intent to adjust the PBF allocation to a specific institution relative to its performance. The third level of assessment occurs at the institutional level, where universities evaluate their performance in relation to selected peers and progress towards their strategic goals. The metrics used in the second and third assessment levels may co-exist but not fully overlap, thus when publicly funded institutions have PBF requirements they need to separately report on, and integrate where possible, both sets of KPIs. Although not usually identical, institutional KPIs should not be in conflict with PBF metrics, otherwise there may be funding consequences.

The challenge in selecting institutional KPIs is to capture the breadth of academic programmes and activities, the outcomes of research and scholarship, and their impact on the community. Performance measures that are relevant to multiple stakeholders balance quantitative and qualitative dimensions of progress, and reflect different aspects of the organisation. Each metric should be aligned with the main pillars of the strategic plan (e.g., teaching and learning, research and scholarship, community engagement) as well as inputs, outputs, or outcomes. Input indicators measure the level of resources used to obtain an output or outcome. Output indicators are quantitative and qualitative measurements of a programme, process, or service; while outcome indicators measure results, such as new knowledge. All of these types of measures are important, as they provide feedback essential to achieving the goals of the strategic plan (Kinnerley, 2018; Selzer, 2018).

Once KPIs are finalised and a data collection and analysis protocol are in place, peer comparator data is integrated into the analysis. This process is led by the executive team with support from institutional analysts. A critical step is to establish the institution's rank relative to peers to allow for benchmarking, year-over-year tracking, and the setting of institutional targets for improvement. The number of institutions selected for benchmarking should be limited to five to 10 for clarity and tracking, and should remain constant through the strategic planning time horizon. Criteria for selecting a peer comparison group are size, geographic location, research intensity, and academic programming.

Regardless of whether the institution plans to benchmark its performance against local, national, or international peers, a comparison group that aligns with the institution's mandate should be selected. Smaller undergraduate universities might select KPIs that allow them to benchmark their performance against local or regional institutions. Large, research-intensive institutions might select measures that benchmark their performance against national and international peer institutions.

A useful resource for identifying appropriate comparator institutions is the Carnegie Classification of Institutions of Higher Education (Indiana University School of Education, 2018), which places colleges and universities in the United States into one of six categories: doctoral universities, master's colleges and universities, baccalaureate colleges, baccalaureate/associate's colleges, associate's colleges, special focus institutions, and tribal colleges. Many other countries have organisations that create networks of similar institutions, such as those that focus on research-intensity, or have degree-granting status. Table 5.4 gives some examples of these networks by jurisdiction.

Table 5.4 Examples of University Networks by Jurisdiction

Country	Organisation	Membership
East Asia	Association of East Asian Research Universities (AEARU)	• 17 research-intensive universities
Australia	Group of Eight (Go8) Universities Australia	• 8 research-intensive universities • 39 degree-granting universities
Canada	Universities Canada The U15	• 96 degree-granting universities • 15 research-intensive universities
China	C9 League	• 9 research-intensive universities
Europe	League of European Research Universities (LERU)	• 23 research-intensive universities
Germany	U15	• 15 research-intensive universities
Japan	RU11	• 11 research-intensive universities
United Kingdom	Russell Group	• 24 research-intensive universities
United States	Association of Public Land Grant Universities (APLU)	• 242 public universities
	Association of American Universities (AAU)	• 65 research-intensive universities

The process to develop and select KPIs should be led by the executive team (PVPA in particular), with oversight by the president. Since an institution's leaders, faculty, and staff are all accountable for progress, they need to be involved in the selection of KPIs; consultation through dialogue and feedback from leaders (e.g., deans, associate vice presidents), the board, and academic senate is required. The chosen KPIs should provide a framework to monitor the strategic plan by balancing efficiency, effectiveness, and user perception measures. Approval of the KPIs by the institution's governing bodies is required since they will be used to assess and communicate performance against goals.

KPIs cannot fully capture the progress of an institution towards its strategic goals. Although they provide a strong foundation to analyse and describe critical quantitative measures and milestones, they do not capture how progress was made. This can be done through qualitative means, or storytelling, showcasing major achievements by students, faculty, staff, or the institution as a whole. This is discussed further in Chapter 6.

Driving the Operational Plan

Once the operational plan is developed and linked to the institutional strategy, the line-of-sight concept is continued by breaking down the five-year plans into one-year segments through the development of annual business plans which contain actions and deliverables. The president needs to create the appropriate links between "what is to be done" and "who is doing it" using a strong accountability framework. While the board has oversight of the strategy and the president's role in executing the strategy, the president needs to ensure that members of the executive team and their portfolios have the appropriate delegation, resources, and support. As shown in Table 5.5, two actions drive the operational plan: the development of an annual business plan and the linking of leadership performance to strategic goals and their execution. These are discussed further in this chapter.

Table 5.5 Driving the Operational Plan

Actions	Outcome
• Development of an annual business plan to implement priorities and allocate resources in alignment with the operational plan • Development of a framework to link leadership performance to strategic goals	Resources and performance linked to strategy execution

Developing the Annual Business Plan

As shown in Figure 5.1, the strategy and operational plan are on five-year time horizons, usually offset by approximately one year since the development of the operational plan commences after the strategy is approved. These documents set the framework for the major pieces of work to be completed during the period of the strategic plan. However, they do not provide details describing what will be done each year and the specific resources required. This level of detail is contained in the annual business plan.

Boards expect to review and approve a business plan each year so they can fulfil their fiduciary responsibility and delegate authority to the president to run the organisation. As part of the business plan, the executive team develops a budget which allocates resources to support salaries, invest in student services, embark on new programmes or initiatives, and maintain and build facilities. This budget is submitted to the board for approval.

For many public institutions, the annual business plan is submitted, after board approval, to the government department overseeing higher education. In this case, the format and structure of the business plan may be predetermined by the government department. Although the business plan is constrained by government requirements, it is important to ensure there are clear links between the activities, budget, and strategic plan.

While every university has an annual business plan to guide short-term operational decisions and investments, what is often missing is a clear linkage of this business plan back to the strategy to create line-of-sight between short-term decisions and long-term goals. In many cases, business plans do not explicitly reflect in plain language how the ongoing work, decisions, and allocated funds support the institution's goals and priorities. Without this connection, key stakeholders can become confused and disengage from the strategy.

In addition to linking long-term strategy to short-term decisions, a business plan should allow for adjustments due to unexpected events and disrupters. These may include fluctuations in the economy or labour market, new government legislation or policies, or geopolitical events impacting student enrolment. In these cases, the business plan should be the shock absorber so the overall strategic plan is not compromised. Resilience is built by monitoring external trends for unexpected circumstances; and when disruptions occur working with the board in adjusting the operational and business plans. A strategy rarely unfolds exactly as anticipated, and the business plan provides agility in allowing for annual adjustments and course correction (Green, 2012).

It is important to build accountabilities for leaders by using the business plan to drive their units' activities. There should be coherency between the business plan and the performance plans of the president and the executive team, which is further discussed in the following section. In addition those in support functions, including human resources, information technologies (IT), finance, and facilities can only support the strategic goals if there are clear links between the business plan and strategy. When this connectivity does not exist the work in these units is solely focused on the activities in their particular silos.

While a business plan is primarily focused on the upcoming year, the 1+2 concept uses a three-year moving window to forecast detailed information about the institution's student enrolment plan, its workforce plan, new programmes being developed, capital infrastructure projects under development, information technology plans, and research programmes and investments.

The budget is a key component of the annual business plan. It gives detailed financial information on the institution's projected revenue and expenditures based on assumptions about the economy (e.g., inflation and exchange rates), student enrolments, and salary increases. Since the budget effectively translates the strategy into the bottom line, it must be carefully constructed to align with institutional priorities. Development of the institutional budget is overseen by the president with particular leadership by the PVPA and the Vice President (Finance and Administration) (VPFA). Once budget parameters have been developed and modelled through assumptions of various itemised costs and revenues, a process to build the budget is initiated.

The alignment of resources to the institutional strategy is one of the key challenges in strategic plan execution (Goldstein, 2012). Unless a rigorous approach is used, there will be conflicting demands for resources and an inability to articulate why some investments are made and others not. Disciplined leadership is needed so resources are not shifted in an ad hoc manner to address constituent concerns, or from higher to lower priorities.

Budgeting in higher education institutions is particularly difficult due to fixed costs tied to salaries, which are not easily reduced or transferred between faculties and units. The creation of a strategic initiatives fund to invest in specific programmes that best support strategic goals is often used to manage this issue (Goldman & Salem, 2015). Further details on higher education budget development can be found in Barr and McClellan (2018).

Linking to Leadership Performance

Clarity of expectations and accountabilities for the president and executive team is increased when the business plan aligns with the strategy. It is important that leadership performance goals are also aligned to strategic outcomes and that leaders are incentivised to deliver on these goals. There is extensive literature on how tracking leadership performance through a structured performance management process helps promote organisational change (e.g., Smither & London, 2009). This process consists of a number of steps, starting with knowledge of the strategic goals, to performance planning, execution, assessment, review, and renewal (Aguinis, 2009). The intent herein is not to cover the full spectrum of the performance management process; instead, the focus is on one specific step, which is the development of the performance plan framework for the president and executive leadership team, once the strategic goals are in place. This step encapsulates the conversion of strategy to concrete actions, results, and achievements, so there is accountability on leaders to ensure their efforts are targeted effectively.

Presidential performance plans are developed and assessed annually, so the board can provide input and oversight on the president's performance relative to the institutional strategy. There should therefore be line-of-sight between the strategy, the operational plan, the annual business plan, and the president's goals and actions. In turn, the president ensures that the executive team's performance plans are coordinated and linked to these documents. This process is then cascaded throughout the institution.

Many templates exist to construct a performance plan, and Table 5.6 gives an example for an executive team member. On the left, the key portfolio goals for the year are listed. All of the activities in the executive's portfolio—especially the day-to-day work—do not need to be included in the performance plan as this creates an unmanageable document. The plan should contain four or five broad goals, with some potentially taking two or more years to complete and requiring new actions each year.

The second column contains a listing of the operational plan priorities that the work will support, and this may be one priority or several, depending on the goal. The third column comprises the actions, what specifically will be done, and these need to be measurable. The nature of the measurement is contained in the subsequent column and may be quantitative: "increase

Table 5.6 Executive Team Member Performance Plan Structure

Portfolio Goal	Operational Plan Priorities Supported	Actions	Metrics/ Deliverables	Cross-Portfolio Support Required	Results
List of goals to be addressed during the year (some goals may take several years with new actions each year).	Priorities from the operational plan to be supported through the actions (one goal may support more than one priority).	Actions to be undertaken to deliver on the goal. These need to be clear and measurable.	Metrics or deliverables for each action so that the level of success or completion can be assessed.	Support required by other Executive Team Portfolios.	Results relative to the actions and metrics. These are formally reported annually with a semi-annual check-in.

health research funding by 10%," or it may be a deliverable: "completion and approval of a revised student admission policy."

"Cross-Portfolio Support Required" is included since many goals and actions cannot be completed without support, such as time and resources, from other executive portfolios. It is important that the leaders of these portfolios have agreed to allocate the resources accordingly, otherwise the work of the executive and their team will be compromised. Finally, the right-hand column documents the results so progress can be assessed during the evaluation phase.

Development of these performance plans is done by each executive team member after significant consultation within their own teams and with the president. They should review each other's plans to ensure that the cross-portfolio support is clear and budgeted for, and that the overall pace for the year is manageable. One of the benefits of this review is that capacity issues may become evident; and can be dealt with, possibly by postponement of certain goals or actions, at a later time, before the performance plans are finalised.

In addition to the structure presented in Table 5.6, an executive team's performance plan can include shared team goals. The inclusion of three to five team goals, that are pan-institutional and derived from the strategic plan or an employee engagement survey, can drive a strong team culture (Heslin, Carson & VandeWalle, 2009). An example of a team goal is "embed entrepreneurial thinking into the institutional culture"; with each team member held accountable for actions appropriate to their portfolio.

For executive team members, performance plans are formally reviewed with the president twice per year; at a semi-annual check-in and during the team member's annual evaluation. This is in addition to the regularly scheduled meetings a president will have with their team members—individually and collectively—throughout the year on various files, issues, and progress.

A template for a president's performance plan is provided in Table 5.7. It is similar to the performance plan for executive members, albeit a slightly modified version since the president's responsibilities are institution-wide. It includes five to seven goals, actions, metrics/deliverables, and results.

Table 5.7 President's Performance Plan Structure

Goal	Actions	Metrics/ Deliverables	Results
List of five to seven goals to be addressed during the year. These should directly address strategy and culture.	Actions to be undertaken to deliver on the goal. These need to be clear and measurable.	Metrics or deliverables for each action so that the level of success or completion can be assessed.	Results relative to the actions and metrics. These are formally reported annually with a semi-annual check-in.

The goals should be tied directly to executing strategy and enhancing an effective institutional culture (discussed in Chapter 6). The president's annual performance plan should be approved and then formally reviewed twice per year, normally by a committee of the board. This is in addition to regular updates to the board (and board committees) and meetings with the board chair. Often a summary of the annual performance plan is publicly available for transparency.

Execution of the strategic plan needs to be top of mind not only throughout an academic institution, from the leadership to the clerical staff, but also for the board and the academic senate. Each governing body has numerous standing committees that collectively receive, deliberate, and approve new policies, programmes, or budgets as well as oversee risks. The coordination of these activities, and the alignment of the work to support the institutional strategy, is complex. It involves the president and their executive team, as well as the university secretariat.

A clear strategic plan, supported by the operational and annual business plans, leads to a more organised and coherent approach to the flow of work of the governing bodies. Meeting agendas for these bodies can be planned in advance through the development of work plans, to preclude the ad hoc delivery of items. Some items on these work plans are the regular work that is performed at certain times each year (e.g., review of financial statements), and other items are strategic or operational according to the annual business plan. In combination, they indicate the scope of work to be done, recognising that unanticipated items may emerge during the year. Table 5.8 shows an example of how a work plan is constructed.

Table 5.8 Work Plan for a Board or Academic Senate

Committee Chair: [name1] Committee Vice Chair: [name2] Responsible Executive: [name3]	Meeting 1 ... Meeting 4	Responsible Executive
Each item to be considered over the year should be listed. Some of these items will be key responsibilities of the committee as per the terms of reference, and others will be strategic or operational items that emerge from the business plan which are specific to that year.	Each item will include the amount of time needed on the agenda for the meeting in which it is being considered.	Title of the responsible executive for each item on the work plan should be listed.
Total Meeting Time (min)	Length of each meeting can be tabulated based on the time required for each item on the meeting work plan.	

Summary

The most difficult aspect of strategy development is its execution, since this is when tough decisions need to be made. Successful conversion to tangible results and outcomes takes committed and sustained effort, requiring integration into all levels of decision-making. Although the president has a key leadership role to play in strategy execution, ownership and accountability across the institution is needed. Table 5.9 summarises the key concepts in Chapter 5.

Table 5.9 Chapter Summary: Executing the Strategy

- Conversion of a strategy into tangible results and outcomes takes committed and sustained effort; the status quo is reinforced if the strategy is not put into action.
- Visibility between strategic goals, the pathway to achieve goals, the pace at which the work will progress and the responsibilities of key individuals and bodies, allows the president to "simplify complexity" and demonstrate how the strategy is being delivered.
- Two steps form strategy execution: converting strategy to operations through the development of an operational plan and selection of KPIs, and implementation of the operational plan through the creation of an annual business plan and linkage to a leadership performance framework.
- An operational plan is developed and structured so it can be actioned. A consultative model grounded in inclusivity is required to develop the plan since it is where the "rubber hits the road" and stakeholders have a significant interest in its outcome.
- An operational plan includes priorities, objectives, timelines, and KPIs. The number of priorities should be limited to three to five for ease of understanding and communication.
- Evaluating and reporting progress requires a set of performance metrics. KPIs allow for evaluation, monitoring progress, and benchmarking, thus providing accountability and a scorecard for the board in its oversight of strategy and the president's performance.
- The annual business plan guides short-term operational decisions and investments, and creates line-of-sight between these decisions and longer-term goals. Without connectivity, stakeholders become confused and may disengage from the strategy.
- A business plan can act as a shock absorber for unexpected events and disrupters without compromising the overall strategic plan. A strategy rarely unfolds exactly as anticipated, and this provides agility in allowing for annual adjustments and course correction.
- A rigorous approach to budgeting ensures resources are not shifted in an ad hoc manner to address constituent concerns, or from higher to lower priorities. Higher education institutions have fixed costs which are not easily reduced or transferred between faculties and units.
- Performance plans for the president and executive team encapsulate the conversion of strategy to concrete actions, results, and achievements so there is accountability on leaders to ensure that their efforts are targeted effectively.
- Execution of the strategic plan includes the work of the board and the academic senate. Having a clear strategic plan, supported by the operational and annual business plan, allows for a more organised and coherent approach to the work flow of the governing bodies.

6 Future-Proofing

Once a strategic direction is identified and initiated, consistent and sustained effort must be made to monitor progress towards strategic goals. This can only be done if the strategy becomes part of the "DNA" of the organisation and is broadly understood, endorsed, and actioned. This is the concept of future-proofing—using the strategy to maintain a focus on the future while mitigating the impact of unforeseen events.

To maintain the focus on strategy within the institution, stakeholders must be kept aware of the progress towards the institution's strategic goals. Communication—of decisions, investments, achievements, and impacts and how they are linked to the institutional strategy—is one of the most important aspects of executing a strategic plan. If done well, it develops and harnesses the energy and commitment of stakeholders on and off campus. If done poorly, it results in a lack of understanding and buy-in on what the strategic plan is meant to accomplish, and leads to an overall failure of the strategic plan (Tierney & Lanford, 2018).

A second key component in driving strategy is institutional culture. Relative to the corporate sector, research into institutional culture within the higher education sector has been limited, but there are several studies which define and show the importance of culture in transformational change (Kezar & Eckel, 2002; Taye, Sang & Muthanna, 2019). Institutional culture can be defined as:

> persistent patterns of norms, values, practices, beliefs, and assumptions that shape the behavior of individuals and groups in a college or university and provide a frame of reference within which to interpret the meaning of events and actions on and off the campus.
>
> (Kuh & Whitt, 1988:p.6)

Kuh & Whitt (1988) argue that institutional culture is a process that shapes—and is shaped by—interactions amongst stakeholders inside and outside the institution, and is also a product reflective of organisational structures, traditions, and history.

Tierney and Lanford (2018) conclude that institutional culture is not easily defined as it is both subjective, with different actors having varying and complex perceptions, and not easily captured through organisational charts and quantitative measures. In support of this conclusion the authors note, "institutional culture in higher education is perhaps most apparent when individuals move to a new campus environment after spending a significant amount of time at a single college or university" (Tierney & Lanford, 2018:p.2). The relationships, expectations, procedures, and practices vary between institutions and "it takes considerable time for an individual to comprehend the intricate web of relationships and routines that constitute institutional culture" (Tierney & Lanford, 2018:p.2). Moreover, they argue that the organisational environment of higher education is socially constructed by individuals from a wide range of backgrounds and disciplines who value vigorous debate and critique as a fundamental component to gain a deeper understanding.

The importance of nurturing and harnessing institutional culture as an enabler of the strategy, can be seen in those institutions that make great strides in their strategic direction compared to those that do not. Similarly, leaders who act on assumptions about an institution's culture without understanding its nuances and its differences to other institutions will experience negative consequences. As discussed by Tierney and Lanford (2018), crises in higher education institutions are often caused by presidents or boards transgressing the boundaries of institutional culture, resulting in confusion and conflict about shared values. Several studies have identified positive relationships between institutional performance and organisational culture (Omerzel, Biloslavo & Trnavcevic, 2011; Trivellas & Dargenidou, 2009). Higher education studies have investigated this relationship, from the perspectives of the type of institutional culture that needs to be fostered to promote change, to the impact that change has on institutional culture (Kezar & Eckel, 2002). As noted by Hinton (2012),

> The impact of institutional culture on strategic planning cannot be overestimated. In fact, if you gave the same strategic plan to ten different institutions, those institutions would each interpret the plan differently and develop ten different implementation plans. These differences are usually the result of at least three critical factors: the institution's unique environment (including the institutional mission and history of the organisation); the structure and competence of the administrative staff of the institution; and, the development of staff commitment to planning.
> (p.23)

The levels of commitment and investment by an institution's faculty and staff—and their perception of whether the institution is invested in them and their futures—influences the speed and impact of strategy implementation. Tierney (1988:p.5) states that "a central goal of understanding organisational culture is to minimise the occurrence and consequences of cultural conflict and help foster the development of shared goals." The loss of key employees due to institutional culture issues is well known and a risk to organisations, especially when driving transformational change (Daimler, 2018). Without overstating the importance of culture, it is truly the "secret sauce" for success.

The symbiosis between transformational change and institutional culture is shown in Figure 6.1. Both sides of the figure are critical to the successful adoption, implementation, and overall impact of an institution's strategic plan. The left side of the figure illustrates the linkage between strategic priority implementation, measurement of results through KPIs, and communication of impacts to stakeholders. This process is important as it connects the decisions made in executing the strategy and results obtained with individuals who need to commit to, and participate in, the institution's journey. Similarly, as shown on the right side of the figure, institutional culture needs to be analysed and broadly communicated, and as discussed further in this chapter, those who are responsible for the development of action plans for improvement should be held accountable.

Both elements in Figure 6.1 operate as flywheels that are in continuous motion. They are also synergistic to one another: a clear strategy provides a

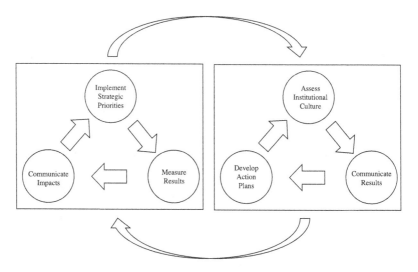

Figure 6.1 Strategy Implementation and Culture Enhancement Flywheels

framework to support an effective institutional culture, and a focus on culture drives the organisation's values and norms, which reinforce the institutional strategy and build a collective commitment for change rather than complacency.

Five key principles lead to an effective linking of strategy and culture: (1) informed consultation, (2) recognition and reinforcement of the institution's value proposition, (3) transparency of decision criteria, (4) clear and consistent communication, and (5) accountability of leaders to the institution's strategic goals and values. This chapter focuses on delivering consistent communication about the strategic plan and its progress, as well as enhancing the institution's culture to drive stakeholder commitment and support transformational change. These two steps comprise Phase 5 of the strategic planning process, which is highlighted in Table 6.1. Figure 6.2 illustrates the components of future-proofing which are discussed in the following sections.

Table 6.1 Phase 5 of Five-Phase Strategic Planning Process

Phase 1: Setting the Stage	*Phase 2: Informed Engagement*	*Phase 3: Creating the Strategy*	*Phase 4: Executing the Strategy*	*Phase 5: Future-Proofing*
A. Dialoguing with stakeholders	A. Building an engagement platform	A. Developing the strategy	A. Converting strategy to operations	A. Communicating strategic impacts
B. Establishing legitimacy	B. Consulting with stakeholders	B. Building identity and awareness	B. Driving the operational plan	B. Enhancing an effective institutional culture

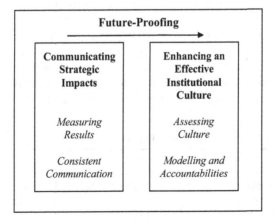

Figure 6.2 Components Supporting Future-Proofing

Communicating Strategic Impacts

One of the most important aspects of implementing a strategic plan is measuring results. Strategic plans are meant to transform (or at a minimum evolve) an organisation, so the ability to determine if progress is being made is crucial. Stakeholders want to see that the strategy is working and making a difference, otherwise they will disengage and retreat to the status quo. Once the results (quantitative and qualitative) are measured, they should be integrated into consistent communications with stakeholders. As shown in Table 6.2, leaders need to measure and communicate the ongoing impact of the strategy to ensure stakeholders remain committed to the strategic priorities.

Measuring Results

What gets measured to reflect the progress and impact of a strategic plan is important since it forms the basis for the narrative on the health, advancement, and growth of the institution. Chapter 5 discussed the development of KPIs to provide a quantitative framework for the overall performance of an institution as well as progress towards strategic goals. As was noted, definition and selection are critical since KPIs are a tangible representation of the institution's progress in implementing the strategic plan. When KPIs are not linked to the strategy a loss of focus and accountability will result, which is a risk within large, complex institutions, such as universities. Regular updates of KPIs—usually on an annual basis—keep stakeholders apprised of progress as well as benchmarking relative to peer institutions. Internal tracking and analysis may be done at a higher frequency.

Limiting the measurement and communication of the strategic plan progress and impact to KPIs alone can lead to a loss of commitment to the strategy. Academic institutions are inherently diverse in people, disciplines and communities of interest, so capturing impacts through numbers alone does not suffice. An academic institution should enable and empower people and communities, so exemplars of success through qualitative means naturally complement quantitative KPIs. The narrative of the institution must

Table 6.2 Communicating Strategic Impacts

Actions	Outcome
• Measurement of strategic impacts using quantitative and qualitative means • Consistent communication of impacts by leaders to stakeholders	Ongoing stakeholder alignment to the strategy

also include the achievements of its students, faculty, staff, and alumni who are its builders, champions, and ambassadors. Stories capture an emotion and build a connection that KPIs cannot replicate, and they are extremely powerful tools to animate the strategy to stakeholders. Fortunately, stories of achievement through student or faculty awards, research achievements, teaching innovation, or philanthropic investments are abundant within academic institutions. They can be used to highlight and profile progress of the strategic plan on a continuous basis in formats relevant to particular stakeholder groups.

A potential difficulty when measuring and communicating progress on the strategic plan is managing expectations, especially the time needed for visible results. Some actions will produce quick results, such as changes in personnel or structures within the institution, or the creation of task forces to deliver recommendations in a particular area; but generally, it will take two to three years to realise the full impact of a strategic plan. It may only be then that stakeholders (even those internal to the institution) will realise that the organisation is moving forward as intended. Maintaining alignment during this time is crucial as discussed further in this chapter. Given KPIs and qualitative stories are the primary means to measure and report progress, a critical question is "How do they impact the perception and reputation of the institution?" Perceptions of the institution and its reputation for alumni, teaching, and research are its currency, so critical outcomes of the strategic plan are improvements in both. Unfortunately, changes in these factors (especially reputation) are on an even longer timeline than other identified outcomes. Improving perceptions of the institution necessitates stakeholders changing their mental image of the organisation, which may have been locked in years (or decades) earlier. This process takes careful, constant, and consistent effort. An institution's reputation is also based on rankings, which are often weighted towards research outcomes, and any improvements in these activities occur over multiple years.

Measurement of perceptions and reputation of the institution can occur in parallel with KPIs. Surveys every two or three years can provide information on progressive changes. If possible, the first survey should be done in conjunction with the launch of the strategic plan to establish a baseline. Alternative surveys may be administered to different external audiences depending on what is to be measured and analysed. For example, a broad reputational survey targeting the public gives a macro view of how the community (local, regional, or national) perceives the institution, and whether the public view is aligned with how the institution sees itself and the image it is trying to project through its strategy. In addition, it can provide valuable information on how the public views the institution relative to its peers. By definition, the public includes parents who are significant influencers on which institutions their children attend. Institutional reputation is a key factor influencing this decision. Over time this type of survey will provide feedback as to the effectiveness of communications strategies and marketing campaigns tied to the strategy.

More targeted surveys can assess how specific stakeholders, such as alumni and government, perceive the institution and whether this perception is changing. Alumni are normally an institution's most fervent champions, so it is important to understand whether they are incentivised to stay up to date on activities and progress, and to be ambassadors for future students and philanthropy. They are also an important group to measure whether the institution's communications are being heard and absorbed.

For public institutions, a survey of government leaders (elected and unelected officials at municipal, provincial/state, and federal levels) to ascertain their perception of the institution and its strategy gives valuable feedback on whether the messages and priorities are consistent (over time and from all institutional leaders) and are effective in driving performance and accountability. In the current age of performance-based funding for public institutions, having clarity and consistency from the institution as a means to differentiate itself in the marketplace will have a direct impact on resource investments from the government. Ensuring government leaders understand the strategy, its impact, and the accountability framework surrounding it, is essential when making the case for investment in a resource-constrained environment.

Donors are another key stakeholder group for whom perception and reputation matter. Often a fundraising campaign will be developed and launched in conjunction with a new institutional strategy. The ability to attract additional resources to help execute the strategy through investments in students, research, programmes, and infrastructure is particularly significant, given reductions in government support, in many jurisdictions, for value-added initiatives. In the lead-up to a campaign, a survey of key donors can provide information on their views of the institution's leaders and its strategy, which can inform the level of support that can be expected in terms of donor investment and hence the overall size of the campaign goal. The donor community is thus an important bellwether for the institution in terms of gauging changing perceptions.

An institution's placement in the international and national ranking indices is partially based on its reputation. As an example, several global university rankings use reputational surveys for 30 to 40% of the weight of the final scores (Pavel, 2015). Thus it is important to continually monitor how the strategy is influencing the institution's reputation. Some universities have dedicated teams tasked with driving improved results in reputational surveys.

Table 6.3 Measurement Tools and Outcomes to Assess Strategy

Measurement Tool	Information Provided	Attributes of Collected Information	Stakeholder Interest	Outcome
Key Performance Indicators	• Progress on selected measures • Benchmarking with other institutions • Direct assessment of strategy	• Annual measure • Narrow assessment of progress • Negative and positive information	• Board • Senior leadership • Internal stakeholders • Government • Donors • Ranking organisations	Reputation
Narratives	• Achievements of internal stakeholders • Indirect assessment of strategy	• Continuously collected • Positive information • Reflects multiple outcomes of strategy	• Board • Internal stakeholders • Alumni and donors • Community • Government	Motivation and commitment Building of internal connections
Surveys	• Stakeholder perceptions • Impact of strategy on external stakeholders	• Perceptions • Bi-annual collection • Negative and positive information	• Board • Senior leadership team • Development professionals • Marketing professionals	Improved communication and engagement with stakeholders

Table 6.3 summarises the various measurement tools to assess strategic progress and impact as well as the expected outcomes. Specific communication channels and forums are discussed in the following section.

Consistent Communication

Measuring the progress and impacts of a strategic plan is important; but equally important is communication of the results to stakeholders. As discussed earlier, communication of decisions, investments, achievements, and impacts—and how they are linked to the institutional strategy—must be constant and consistent, since research has shown that repetitive communication is needed for people to absorb and understand key messages (Cornett, 2019). This is particularly true when considering a strategic plan and its results, since there are many audiences and modes of communication that must be considered. To emphasise this point, Tierney and Lanford (2018) discuss two key administrative behaviours that have the potential to instill a sense of stability and confidence within an institution: the first is an adherence to an institutional identity and the second is the maintenance of effective communication channels.

The goals of stakeholder communication are to collectively inform, inspire, and activate. It is not sufficient to merely transmit information since successful implementation of a strategic plan relies on continuous buy-in and call to action. Stakeholders need to be confident that the institutional strategy is building a sustainable future if they are to continue supporting and investing in the university's activities.

At face value, communication of the outcomes and impacts of a strategic plan appears straightforward. There may be designated opportunities or events throughout the institution's annual calendar that are geared towards updates on progress, and a natural assumption is these will create the level of awareness needed to keep stakeholders aligned and motivated. However, given the complexity of academic institutions, the enormous flow of information that stakeholders are exposed to on a daily basis, and in some cases, the level of cynicism about the need for and relevance of strategic plans in the first place, ongoing communication involving the strategic plan and its impacts requires sensitivity and consistent effort. Effective communication requires developing the appropriate messages for the different key audiences. And it requires the visibility of leaders "walking the talk."

Given the numerous dimensions of an academic institution, communicating the impact of a strategic plan should rely on the notion of "simplifying complexity." Information overload is a significant risk and is detrimental to effective messaging. Trying to capture the entirety of the institution in one fell swoop is bound to fail; instead, the focus should be on three to five key messages at a time. These can be tailored to a specific audience or community of interest. For example, faculty members are often interested in teaching innovations or research achievements, while students are interested in classroom upgrades, new academic programmes, or increased scholarship funding. The key is to draw the line-of-sight from the strategy to these initiatives and achievements, which is what simplifies the message in a complex environment.

The president clearly has an important and defined role in communicating the impact of the strategic plan since they speak for the institution as a whole. In fact, it can be argued that the primary role of the president is to constantly communicate the plans and achievements of the institution, and consistently tie them back to the strategic goals. This latter point is critical.

Merely communicating what is transpiring at the institution—the "what"—without the "why"—that is, the strategic plan—will leave stakeholders disengaged or confused. Repetitive and consistent messaging of the overall narrative cannot be overemphasised. One of the most important roles of the president is supporting the institution's strategy through storytelling. This may be done in one-on-one meetings, small groups, or at large gatherings such as town halls or annual convocations.

Report cards and dashboards are other effective means of communicating information in a timely and compact way. For example, an annual community report should contain both numerous stories highlighting the achievements of the year, and a report card where the KPIs and benchmarks are explicitly included (University of Calgary, 2018a). This provides a level of accountability that is appreciated by stakeholders and funders. Additionally, dashboards can be used to update the board on progress towards institutional goals and priorities.

Although the president has primary responsibility for communicating the strategic plan and its impacts, this task needs to be shared across the institution to reflect broad alignment. Members of the executive team should be committed and active participants in communicating progress. They need to link the strategic plan to their portfolios so their employees can also see a line-of-sight between the institutional strategy, their unit and, ultimately, themselves. Dashboards to report on elements of the operational plans are a useful means of communicating progress. These more granular dashboards can be tied to a particular initiative, research theme, or priority and provide a means to translate progress on recommendations or goals into impacts using metrics and strong visuals to demonstrate advancement.

Other leaders across the institution such as deans, departmental chairs, associate vice presidents, and directors also need to be vocal in linking the strategic plan to the work being performed in their units, particularly given that they have "enhanced legitimacy due to their academic backgrounds" (Tierney & Lanford, 2018:p.5). To achieve a "daisy chain" of communication from one level down to the next level of leadership, it is recommended that various units within the institution develop their own sub-strategies which are visibly linked to the institutional strategy. A university has several faculties or schools, and these differ in size, academic programmes, research focus, and community impact. Thus, the way in which each of these units contributes to the institutional strategy will also vary.

While the institutional strategy provides a broad framework for expectations and key parameters for performance, a unit sub-strategy harnesses its particular capacity to contribute to the campus-wide goals. Sub-strategies provide localisation of the institutional strategy, which creates greater relevance at the individual level. This is important since one of the largest challenges in the implementation of a strategy is having faculty and staff understand its impact on them and how they can individually contribute to the strategy. Informal leaders, who understand and support the strategy, are critical in cascading the strategy into lower levels of the institution. They are defined as individuals who "do not hold a specific leadership position, yet are recognised as dependable individuals who represent positions on behalf of others" (Tierney & Lanford, 2018:p.5). Informal leaders are able to contextualise strategic goals in terms of their impact on a given unit. They are a key element in integrating the strategy into faculty and unit decisions, as their colleagues listen and follow their guidance.

Table 6.4 reviews the numerous modes to communicate the progress and results of a strategic plan, as well as the intended audiences/stakeholders and frequency. This is a non-exhaustive list but it illustrates that communication is a shared responsibility at all levels of the organisation. Development of the identified documents and events should be led by the strategic communications team, with input from the president and executive team members.

Table 6.4 Communication Strategies for Progress and Impacts of the Strategic Plan

Communication Mode	Stakeholders	Frequency
Community Report (document)	• All	Annual
Community Report (presentations)	• Internal stakeholders • External stakeholders	Annual
Town Halls	• Faculty, staff, and students (may be separate)	2–3 times per year
Campus E-newsletter	• Internal stakeholders (faculty, staff, board)	Daily
One-on-One Meetings	• Key donors • Elected government officials • Senior government officials	Ongoing
Dashboards	• Board • Donors • Government	Quarterly
External E-newsletter	• Alumni • Donors • Community Leaders	Monthly
Progress on Operational (Academic and Research) Plan	• Faculty, staff, and students • Mid-level government officials	Annual with ongoing updates as appropriate

Enhancing an Effective Institutional Culture

As discussed previously, the importance of an effective institutional culture in driving strategy cannot be underestimated. There is significant literature on how culture differentiates one organisation from another and acts as a management system that requires constant attention (Korman, 2019). As discussed in Chapter 3, developing the institutional strategy through a comprehensive and engaging process helps shape organisational culture by being transparent about the values to which the institution aspires. Active engagement during the strategic planning phase provides a foundation for the transition from strategy development to execution. It also leads to motivated stakeholders who have invested their intellectual—and often emotional—capacity into defining the institution's future state. They have made significant investments of time and energy through their active involvement in the engagement process, and want to ensure their investment leads to a sustainable university. Chapter 4 discussed the launch of the strategy as a way of increasing awareness and excitement on campus and in the community. Through a mix of anticipation, pride, and commitment, all constituencies should be ready to embark on the exciting journey of implementing the institutional strategy.

A potential pitfall at this point is the assumption that the energy and passion that led to the development of the institutional strategy can be carried on organically over the years it will take to execute it. This is a natural assumption for the president and the executive team, as they are empowered through their positions and access to resources to drive initiatives forward. They work together, have a strong commitment to the strategy, and assume others are equally committed.

For faculty and staff however, ongoing commitment and investment in the institutional strategy may dissipate, for a number of reasons, including poor strategy execution, poor communication, or a weak institutional culture. Making an effort to maintain and grow commitment to the strategy will often differentiate those institutions which truly make great strides in their strategic direction from those that do not. This requires an overall focus on change management, since leaders are driving the organisation to a new state which, by definition, requires new ways of thinking and operating. It is known from the literature that neglecting the impact of the changes on the institution's culture will lead to limited implementation of the strategy. As Tierney (1991:p.5) states "to implement decisions, leaders must have a full, nuanced understanding of the organisation's culture. Only then can they articulate decisions in a way that will speak to the needs of various constituencies and marshal their support."

Table 6.5 lists the key actions required to increase understanding of, and commitment to, the strategy. If these actions are addressed, in addition to

Table 6.5 Enhancing an Effective Institutional Culture

Actions	Outcome
• Assessment and communication of institutional culture • Ensurance that leaders model and are held accountable to enhance institutional culture	Increased understanding and commitment to the strategy

those in Table 6.2, the expected synergy between the strategy and campus culture will result, as shown in Figure 6.1.

Assessing Culture

There are numerous metrics that reflect the effectiveness of institutional culture. Some of these are straightforward, such as faculty and staff attrition rates, absenteeism, and information gained through exit surveys. The frequency and nature of protected disclosures (e.g., whistleblower complaints) can also point to issues around culture (ICD, 2019). However, given the complexity of higher education institutions, a framework to adequately describe and assess an institution's culture must be multi-dimensional.

Tierney (1991) defines six essential elements of higher education institutional culture and applied this framework to analyse a specific higher education institution. The six elements are mission, environment, socialisation, information, strategy, and leadership—and when considered together—an institutional culture can be assessed. In contrast, Berquist (1992) identifies four institutional archetypes of higher education institutional culture: collegial, managerial, developmental, and negotiating. Kezar and Eckel (2002) used both frameworks to analyse six institutions, and they discovered a relationship between institutional culture and change, suggesting the value of auditing an institutional culture before engaging in a change process. It is emphasised that change strategies that work on one campus may not work on another, and that simply applying universal change principles may result in resistance to any change occurring.

An extensive audit of an institution's culture using one of the frameworks discussed earlier may not be feasible, due to limitations of time and resources. However, an effective alternative is to survey faculty and staff through an employee engagement survey. An engagement survey is not a complete proxy for an assessment of an institution's culture since it only measures an employee's emotional and intellectual connection, and their commitment to the organisation and its strategic direction. Research has shown that engaged employees use greater discretionary effort and are more productive, motivated, innovative, and creative and take more ownership of results, thereby creating and sustaining a high-performing organisation (Chomos, 2017). Although an engagement survey cannot provide a detailed analysis of an institution's culture, it can provide a strong indication of how faculty and staff perceive the organisation and their role in it, which is critical to effectively driving a change process.

Hiring a third-party firm to conduct an employee engagement survey is recommended, as it mitigates concerns that individual feedback may not be held in confidence. These firms also have access to benchmark data from other higher education, or public, institutions, so peer comparisons can be made. Measurement of employee engagement should be done on a regular basis (normally every one to three years) to assess the impact of action plans derived from the previous engagement survey. Pulse surveys, which are surveys of employees that pose fewer, simpler questions to measure the health of the organisation, may be done on a more frequent basis (Welbourne, 2016). If an institution does not have a history of employee engagement surveys, faculty and staff may be skeptical and reluctant to participate at first. A commitment to transparency of the results and follow-up development and implementation of action plans is critical.

The results of an employee engagement survey will provide quantitative and qualitative feedback on employee engagement and enablement. Employee engagement has several definitions in the literature, but generally refers to an employee's emotional connection to the organisation and its goals. It quantifies an employee's commitment as well as the level of discretionary effort that they will contribute to their role, and hence, the institution. Employee enablement refers to the resources, tools, and environment available to an employee that will help them contribute to the organisation's goals (Hyter, 2020).

Factors affecting engagement include whether there is a perceived clear and promising direction, confidence in leadership, individual development opportunities, strong organisational image and reputation, employee respect and recognition, equity, and satisfactory pay and benefits. Factors affecting enablement include the employee's perception of the needed resources to fulfil their role, opportunities for collaboration, access to training, and whether they have the appropriate authority and empowerment for their role (Hyter, 2020).

An organisation's engagement and enablement survey results will only reflect a point in time. Consistency in surveying faculty and staff, transparency in communicating results, and discipline in holding leaders accountable for action should result in improved engagement and enablement over time. Although the goal should be to maximise both engagement and enablement, exceeding the benchmark norms (e.g., higher education sector or public sector) is the desired minimum state. This will demonstrate that relative to its peers, the institution is providing a better environment for its faculty and staff, and that this is driving commitment to the institution and its goals.

From a practical point of view, it is a best practice for the president and the executive leadership team to focus on three or four key areas from the institution-wide employee engagement survey results as part of their annual performance plans (see Chapter 5). This can be done through shared goals among the executive team. This keeps them focused on the main drivers for improved institutional culture, which can be communicated broadly to faculty and staff.

An effective institutional culture is important to harness the aggregate energy and enthusiasm of the campus community for achieving its strategic goals. However, its power will be felt—and indeed tested—during crises or significant disruptions. An effective culture can be utilised and often improved in times of stress or during unforeseen events, when the institution has the resilience to cope, build community, and maintain its long-term focus on the future.

Modelling and Accountabilities

Enhancement of the institutional culture to drive commitment to the organisation and its strategy should be the inspiration for academic leaders' activities, with an overall goal that all leaders, faculty, and staff live the values of the organisation. The critical first step for this is role modelling by campus leaders in words and actions to ensure that the "tone from the top" is both seen and heard. Transparency, integrity, and commitment to communication are three of the key attributes that faculty and staff—as well as other stakeholders on and off campus—will assess in their leaders to determine if there is true dedication to the agreed-upon values. These three attributes involve continuous active listening and engagement to build a strong internal community based on trust.

Building an effective institutional culture relies on the implementation of best practices, such as:

- institutional culture is, and is seen to be, a priority;
- commitment to an effective institutional culture permeates the organisation;
- institutional culture is assessed with the results disseminated across the institution;

- results are available at the unit level so strong exemplars of effective culture can be celebrated and weaker ones supported;
- leaders across the institution are held accountable to an effective culture in their unit and this is part of their annual performance review; and
- leaders are accountable for the development and implementation of action plans to enhance the effective culture in their unit.

Creating specific programmes or initiatives which are reviewed, developed, and implemented to ensure an effective institutional culture should be an ongoing practice. The results of the employee engagement survey can be used as one tool to develop action plans which identify areas of weakness and opportunities for impact. One such action may be the development or expansion of an employee recognition and rewards programme. Another may involve personal development and training programmes so employees feel valued and see a pathway for a long career at the institution and opportunities for growth. Finally, it may include more foundational pieces such as policy development or refreshment in areas, such as protected disclosure and sexual harassment.

An organisation's culture will also be reinforced when recruiting new faculty and staff. It is important that fit with the institutional culture is taken into account as part of the applicant assessment process. Explicitly communicating the institution's values assists in identifying those who may not align to, or appreciate, the existing culture. Although this may not be a reason to reject a particular candidate, especially in academic hiring which is multi-dimensional, it should be specifically identified as a risk factor that may be mitigated through mentoring. Onboarding programmes for new faculty and staff are also critical elements to ensure that the institutional culture is presented and reinforced in a transparent manner.

Summary

Future-proofing is defined as using strategy to maintain a focus on the future while mitigating the impact of unforeseen events. This involves the communication of strategic impacts so stakeholders are aware of progress and alignment to the strategy is maintained. It also includes the assessment and enhancement of institutional culture so it is effective in driving change. Although research into organisational culture within the higher education sector has been limited relative to the corporate world, a number of studies have linked culture to the ability to drive transformational change.

Table 6.6 Chapter Summary: Future-Proofing

- Communicating strategic impacts involves sharing the results of quantitative and qualitative measurements, and consistent communication by leaders to maintain ongoing alignment to the strategy.
- Using KPIs to measure progress and impact of a strategic plan provides focus and accountability, and an ability to benchmark relative to peer institutions.
- Qualitative progress is tracked through the achievements of students, faculty, staff, and alumni, since stories which capture emotion and build connection are powerful tools to animate the strategy.
- Communication of decisions, investments, achievements, and impacts—and how they are linked to the institutional strategy—is one of the most important aspects of executing a strategic plan. Leaders must identify key audiences and the best communication strategies for each one.
- Enhancing an effective institutional culture involves assessing culture since it is unique to an organisation, and leaders modelling and being held accountable to the desired culture increases understanding of, and commitment to, the strategy.
- A strong institutional culture is an enabler of strategy and can differentiate those institutions which truly make great strides in their strategic direction and those that do not.
- Ongoing commitment and investment by faculty and staff in the strategy may dissipate if there is poor strategy execution, poor communication, a weak institutional culture, or all of these.
- A framework that adequately describes and assesses higher education institutional culture is multi-dimensional. Surveying faculty and staff through an employee engagement survey can contribute to better understanding the existing culture.
- An effective institutional culture can be utilised and often improved in times of stress or during unforeseen events, when the institution has the resilience to cope, build community, and maintain its long-term focus on the future.
- Role modelling by campus leaders through words and actions to ensure the right "tone from the top" is important for stakeholders to determine if there is true commitment to the agreed-upon values.
- Leaders across the institution need to be held accountable to an effective culture in their unit and this should be part of their annual performance review. This includes the development and implementation of action plans to enhance the effective culture in their unit.

In particular, the fact that each higher education institution has a unique culture needs to be understood and appreciated since it plays a significant role in why change may occur or not. Table 6.6 gives additional summary points to the future-proofing concept.

Appendix
University of Calgary Case Study

The following case study is based on the development, execution, and impact of strategic planning at the University of Calgary. Background on the Canadian higher education system and the university are given followed by a description of the work done in two separate strategic planning processes, in 2010–2011 and 2016–2017, in alignment with the five phases for strategic planning presented in this book.

Context and Background

In Canada, higher education policy, implementation, and funding are the responsibility of the 13 provinces and territories. Higher education institutions across the country thus operate under different institutional mandate frameworks, funding models, quality assurance systems, and strategic research ecosystems. Most of these institutions are publicly funded with some being private or not-for-profit. There are 96 degree-granting institutions of varying sizes and mandates that are members of Universities Canada, an association providing a voice for Canadian universities, domestically and internationally (Universities Canada, 2020). The history and structure of Canada's decentralised higher education system can be found in Jones (2014).

Notwithstanding provincial and territorial responsibilities, the federal government plays a role in two key areas of higher education. One is direct or indirect student support through scholarships, grants, loan programmes, and funding for skills development. The second is research funding, including infrastructure funding related to research and innovation, through various programmes and agencies. Often federal research and infrastructure support is complementary to provincial funding programmes, and in some cases is dependent on matched provincial investment.

The federal government sets priorities for the development of science and technology (e.g., Government of Canada, 2014), and some federal research investments in higher education are targeted to specific federal priorities or must be aligned to institutional research priorities. Many provincial governments also develop priorities and principles to drive research investment and outcomes for economic or skills development (e.g., Government of Alberta, 2017a). Starting in the late 1990s, the linkage of some federal and provincial research-funding programmes to government or institutional priorities led to the requirement that Canadian universities have a strategic research plan that identifies their areas of priority, excellence, and focus. Over time, the concept of university strategic planning evolved such that strategic research plans were often developed as part of, or a follow-on to, a larger institutional strategic planning process and, in some cases, in conjunction with the development of an institutional academic plan.

The University of Calgary is a young public, research-intensive university which was formally established in 1966. Since that time, it has grown to over 34,000 students and 6,000 faculty and staff across five campuses, including one in Doha, Qatar. The majority of the over 26,000 undergraduate students come from the surrounding region (about 81.3%), with the remainder from the rest of Canada (9.6%) and internationally (9.1%). For the graduate student cohort, approximately 26% are international. The university has 14 faculties comprising over 250 programmes. These include numerous professional programmes such as engineering, business, law, medicine, nursing, social work, education, architecture, planning and landscape, as well as arts, science, and kinesiology. The University of Calgary has a mandate from the Government of Alberta to offer undergraduate and graduate education and to conduct basic and applied research. It is a member of Universities Canada and the U15 group of Canadian research universities (U15, 2020).

The University of Calgary is located in the city of Calgary near the Rocky Mountains in the province of Alberta. With a population of almost 1.6 million, it is Canada's fifth largest census metropolitan area (CMA), with more than 33% of the population belonging to a visible minority group, ranking it third in diversity among major Canadian cities (Government of Alberta, 2017b; Calgary Economic Development, 2020a). According to Census 2016 results, Calgary has the youngest population of major Canadian cities with 70.2% of the population between the ages of 15 to 64, and a median age of 37.2 years (Statistics Canada, 2020). A total of 18% of all graduates in the city have a STEM (science, technology, engineering, mathematics) background, which is the highest for the major CMAs in Canada. The four highest industry groups representing employment are: (1) healthcare and social assistance, (2) professional, science, and technical, (3) retail trade, and (4) finance, insurance, and real estate (Calgary Economic Development, 2020b).

Strategic Planning: 2010–2011

Setting the Stage

In 2010 the University of Calgary did not have a unifying strategic direction, limiting its impact and reputation. Although the university had experienced significant growth in students and research capacity, there were clear signals and a shared concern across stakeholder groups that the institution was not on a path to being sufficiently recognised nationally and internationally for its high-quality academic programmes and research impacts. Additionally, it was felt that the university was not well positioned to compete provincially and federally for operating, research, and infrastructure funding through government or philanthropic investment. Since there was not a broadly endorsed unifying vision guiding priorities and investments, opportunities were missed and potential unrealised. The university also had an impending fiftieth anniversary in 2016 which provided strong motivation to create a sense of urgency around making significant progress.

Early in their tenure, the internally recruited president met with stakeholders in town halls, small groups, and one-on-one sessions, and the feedback was generally consistent. There was some skepticism around the usefulness of strategic plans, however, there was recognition that change was needed. Many internal stakeholders were prepared to support and initiate changes, if a unifying vision and roadmap towards institutional goals were collectively developed. Given the breadth and consistency of feedback at this early stage, the president and the board agreed to initiate a strategic planning process to develop a bold and transformative institutional strategy that would support a major leap forward for the university. This was broadly communicated to stakeholders at various forums and through a document authored by the president which clearly articulated the upcoming process by answering the "why, what, how, who, and when" questions in a succinct format.

A structure to oversee and coordinate the strategic planning process was established in accordance with Figure 2.2 and the discussion in Chapter 2, with the Dean's Council playing an important role to provide input to the process. The strategic oversight committee had 14 members from a cross-section of constituencies and was chaired by a highly respected long-standing faculty member. In this case, the president did not chair the committee, to dispel any perception of undue control; however, it was structured as an ad hoc committee reporting to the president. The working committee had five members with representation from institutional planning, governance, and the president's office along with two business professors with expertise in strategy. A first task for the working committee was to establish a project schedule, timeline, and budget for review by the strategic oversight committee, and approval by the president and board.

Informed Engagement

The development of a communications strategy was led by the working committee and utilised a number of units across the campus with expertise in communications and marketing. The activities listed in Table 3.3 formed the basis of the communications strategy, which included a website to serve as a hub for relevant announcements and documents, and a portal to enrol in focus group discussions.

The working committee coordinated with the university's institutional planning group to develop an environmental scan of the information sources listed in Table 3.4. A PESTLE analysis was used to summarise data, trends, and potential disrupters, and this document could be accessed prior to or during a consultation activity. Links to the multiple documents that informed the environmental scan were included on the website.

As part of the communications plan, the engagement process was branded as "Project Next: We All Decide" (shortened to Project Next). This brand was created to build awareness and excitement with the goal of increasing stakeholder participation. The brand was built through a logo and distinctive colours, which were used on the various communications and consultation materials. It proved to be highly effective at elevating the awareness of the strategic planning process on campus and the community.

Five consultation activities were developed. The primary (and most resource intensive) being focus group sessions as described in Chapter 3. The first focus group was held for board members so they could engage in the process and provide feedback on the consultation strategy. The second group to participate were the deans, so they could champion the process to their constituents. Of the remaining sessions, there were 20 to 30 participants in each with a mixture of faculty, staff, and students. In addition, some sessions were run just for students or external stakeholders. The strategy canvas exercise (see Chapter 3) was used as the consultation tool so comparisons could be made with other institutions regarding areas for improvement and investment. Working committee members trained campus leaders to facilitate the focus group sessions and draw out valuable recommendations while managing faculty and staff expressions of perceived grievances. The strategy canvas allowed facilitators to develop a forward-looking orientation so roadblocks to alignment could be identified.

Internal interest in the consultation processes varied according to perceptions of the degree of impact that the changes in priorities and programmes would have on an individual's work. Some participants initially demonstrated an interest in just being informed, but shifted to more active forms of consultation as this phase progressed. Feedback was collected at the end of each focus group session, and based on an exit survey, over 90% of participants found the sessions to be a positive experience.

A total of 25 focus groups was completed over a period of seven weeks, with 500 individuals participating. Focus groups were held across five themes: (1) student workshops focused on factors enriching the learning environment, (2) research workshops focused on factors strengthening research culture, (3) faculty workshops focused on factors supporting a culture of excellence, (4) staff workshops focused on factors creating a positive work environment, and (5) development workshops focused on creating partnerships with external academic and non-academic organisations.

The remaining four consultation activities were: (1) a "Question of the Week" in the campus e-newsletter where participants were invited to respond to questions on topics ranging from programmes and research to resources and facilities, (2) social media activities to seed conversations, answer questions, provide suggestions, and comment on Project Next, (3) email questions to faculty and staff soliciting comments, ideas, and suggestions, and (4) roving booths which were set up on campus asking students, faculty, and staff their views on potential challenges, inspirational moments, and future plans for the university.

Across all of the engagement platforms, approximately 4,000 stakeholders participated. A summary report of the findings from the consultation phase was sent to all stakeholders by the chair of the oversight committee.

Creating the Strategy

Consultation results were analysed by the working committee through conventional qualitative data analysis techniques, leading to categories and subcategories of recommended changes using the processes discussed in Chapter 4. This information was integrated with the environmental scan information to identify strengths, weaknesses, opportunities, and threats. The summarised information was reviewed by the oversight committee, the president and executive team, senior leaders such as deans, as well as the academic senate and board. The summary included descriptions of the consultation activities, the methodologies used to analyse the data, demographic analyses of participants in relation to the university community, and a SWOT analysis. The information was provided on the website and discussed within faculties and units to provide the broader campus with feedback on what was heard.

The working committee interpreted the information to identify strategic opportunities for the university to improve its impact and reputation in each of the pillars of teaching, research, and community engagement; and also to single out areas in which the university could become a recognised leader. These were assessed and presented to the strategic oversight committee for discussion and selection of the final strategic opportunities—along with the supporting strategic goals—for inclusion in the strategy.

An overarching strategy statement (see Chapter 4) was developed to communicate how the university would increase its impact and build its reputation. This statement, and the strategic goals, were presented to the president and other key groups for feedback and refinement, and after several iterations resulted in the following strategy statement:

> The University of Calgary will be a global intellectual hub located in Canada's most enterprising city. In this spirited, high-quality learning environment, students will thrive in programs made rich by research and hands-on experiences. By our fiftieth anniversary in 2016, we will be one of Canada's top five research universities, fully engaging the communities we both serve and lead.
>
> (University of Calgary, 2011:p.8)

This statement provided a concise description of the value the university would create for its primary communities, the range of programmes that would be supported (scope), and the strategic goal of being a "top five" research university (measurable target) over the next five years. Calgary is known as an entrepreneurial city that prides itself as having an energetic, "can-do" spirit and this is conveyed by stating that the university is located in "Canada's most enterprising city." It also states that student learning will be shaped by research and practical experience. Community engagement is included to clearly signal that it is fundamental to the success of the institution.

Three foundational commitments were made in the strategy: (1) sharpen the focus on research and scholarship, (2) enrich the quality and breadth of learning, and (3) integrate the university with the community. Each of these three commitments was further developed to describe "where we are going" and "how we will get there" over the following five years. Institutional values were also developed and included in the strategy as part of the planning process.

Examples of specific directions in the strategy included: (1) increasing research impact in thematic areas where the university had strength and interest, and as directed by the research community through a task force on research strengths and opportunities, (2) cultivating teaching excellence by integrating research into how teaching is done and how students learn, promoting the professional development of professors, instructors, graduate students, and teaching assistants to create a culture of expert instruction, and (3) becoming a welcoming venue for the exchange of knowledge, for debate, art, culture, sport, and recreational opportunities, ensuring a sense of inclusion and meaningful, productive dialogue and two-way connection to the international landscape of ideas, art, science, and culture for all life-long learners (University of Calgary, 2011).

Once the strategy was finalised, it was approved by the academic senate and board, with the process lasting approximately 10 months from start to end. A communications firm was retained to develop the identity and logo for the strategic plan that supported the brand of the university. The name chosen for the strategy was "Eyes High," which reflected the motto of the university ("I will lift up mine eyes") while being seen as aspirational and forward-looking. A formal launch of the strategy was led by the president to celebrate the conclusion of the process, thank stakeholders, and initiate the strategy execution phase for the period 2011–2016.

An important aspect of the institutional plan was the development of sub-strategies whereby each faculty developed its own strategic plan to contribute to the overall goals of Eyes High. This allowed the deans to align with, and contribute to, the institutional strategy through the work of their faculty, staff, and students, which varied across disciplines. In many cases, these sub-strategic plans captured smaller priority areas which would not rise to the level of institutional prominence, but could be identified and supported at the faculty level. Similarly, some of the non-academic portfolios (e.g., facilities, finance, and services) within the executive team also developed a strategy for their team so they could ensure a line-of-sight between their work and the overall goals of the institution.

Executing the Strategy

The development of an operational plan—split into academic and research plans—was led by the newly recruited PVPA and VPR. The two plans were done in sequence, with the academic plan completed first using the process described in Chapter 5. Seven priorities were included in the academic plan and three priorities formed the research plan, with each being comprised of objectives and timelines. A series of 42 KPIs was selected across the three foundational commitments and benchmarked against five comparator universities. The five highest-ranked research universities in Canada were selected as comparators so progress towards becoming a top-five research institution could be measured. Specific members of the executive team had ownership of various KPIs and were responsible for monitoring and benchmarking prior to an annual roll-up to the institutional level.

Based on the Eyes High strategy, as well as the academic and research plans, annual business plans were developed which articulated annual activities and budgets, as well as forecasts for the following two years, as discussed in Chapter 5. Some of these activities included the development of sub-strategies in key academic (e.g., internationalisation, sustainability, indigeneity, mental health) or research (e.g., energy, chronic disease) areas. Performance plans for the president and executive team were developed in alignment with the business plan and this process was used to cascade to other leaders at the university. A summary of the president's performance plan was published on the university's website. Work plans for the academic senate and board were developed as presented in Table 5.8 and as an effective means to communicate alignment to the strategy.

All of the work to align the strategy with the academic and research plans, as well as business plan and budget, created a line-of-sight needed to "simplify complexity" as discussed in Chapter 5.

Future-Proofing

The impact of the strategic plan was measured through year-over-year and peer comparator benchmarking of the KPIs as well as through various surveys. Alumni surveys assessed perceptions of the university and measured net promoter scores (NPS). All three levels of government were surveyed to determine if the university's strategy and impact were understood; and if the president and leadership team were effective in making the case for investment in the institution. Broader reputational surveys were conducted to measure the local, provincial, and national publics' views of the university and how they compared to its peers. All of these surveys were repeated every two or three years to gauge performance over time.

From the annual assessment of the KPIs, and through the results of these surveys, it was determined that there was an increase in performance throughout the five-year strategic plan period. By 2017, 25 of the 35 KPIs, which had available peer comparator data, were in the top five; with several in the top five on a per-faculty-member basis but not in an absolute sense (e.g., research funding per faculty but not total research funding, which were two separate KPIs). Quantitative and qualitative impacts of the strategy were regularly communicated to stakeholders, by both formal and informal means; including an annual community report, which demonstrated accountability to internal and external stakeholders, and had a positive impact on the reputation of the university (University of Calgary, 2018a).

In addition, dashboards were developed quarterly to report progress on the business plan to the board. Other dashboards were developed to report on progress towards the priorities within the academic and research plans, and these were disseminated to stakeholders on and off campus.

In the early stages of the strategic planning process, it was recognised that the institutional culture needed to shift to being more effective and responsive to trends in the external environment. A campus-wide employee engagement survey was therefore conducted in early 2011 by an external consulting firm to provide baseline data prior to the launch of the strategy and the finalisation of the institution's values. This survey, which was repeated every two years to determine if there were improvements in employee engagement and enablement, was used as part of the assessment of the institution's culture. Results at the institutional level were presented to campus by the president, while the results for each unit were shared by the unit leader, such as a dean.

Initial employee engagement results were poor—as expected based on anecdotal information—and improved significantly over time. Three areas were identified in the first survey and became the focus of the president and the newly formed executive team: (1) building commitment and trust in leadership, (2) ensuring a culture of respect and recognition, and (3) creating a "one university family" environment by building a shared university vision. All the results were shared broadly and action plans were developed for improvement at the institutional and unit levels. These action plans were rolled into annual performance plans for the leadership across the university, including the president.

A key part of developing and implementing an institutional strategy is to increase support from external stakeholders through advice, investment, and reputational growth. In order to obtain resources to deliver on the goals of the Eyes High strategy, a $1.3B CAD fundraising campaign was developed. When launched, this campaign was the third largest for a Canadian public university and was made possible by the community's endorsement of the strategy and donors' beliefs that their investments would make a difference. In particular, key goals and priorities from the strategy, as well as from the academic and research plans, were achieved through philanthropy, including the $40M CAD Taylor Institute for Teaching and Learning and naming of the Cumming School of Medicine for $100M CAD, which was matched by the Government of Alberta for an additional $100M.

Strategic Planning: 2016–2017

Setting the Stage

With the sun setting on the Eyes High strategy in late 2016, a new strategic planning process was launched in coordination with the university's 50th anniversary; which was to be completed and approved by the end of the celebration year in 2017. A key consideration for this process was whether the existing strategy should be retained but updated (evolution), or if an entirely new strategy should be developed to further transform the institution (revolution).

Progress made towards the strategic goals was reviewed in late 2015 along with feedback received through stakeholder meetings on and off campus. This review led to the conclusion that Eyes High was well understood and transforming the university as planned. Based on this result, the president prepared a discussion paper on the background of the original strategy (since many on campus were new so did not have the opportunity to participate in its development), progress made, the idea of an evolutionary approach as well as principles for the process, and other details on structure and timelines. This paper was discussed with the executive team, and then presented and endorsed by the board and academic senate, with agreement that the new strategy should be one of evolution—incremental but important changes to the existing strategy. There was a consensus that introducing an entirely new strategy would have confused stakeholders by signaling that the current direction was not working. There was agreement to consult with stakeholders to update the existing strategy, but with boundaries on the level of change to be made so stakeholder expectations could be managed.

The structure and terms of reference for the strategic oversight committee and working committee closely resembled that used in 2010–2011. A key difference was that in this case, the president chaired the strategic oversight committee since it was not an entirely new strategy. In addition, the working committee was comprised of two members from the 2011 group so there was institutional memory on the process. A project plan and budget were established for the process with the length of time allotted being nine months.

Informed Engagement

Once a communications strategy was created, as described in Chapter 3, environmental summaries were developed for each pillar—teaching, research, and community engagement—to inform faculty, staff, students, and other stakeholders of the progress made on the current strategy. Additional summaries were developed in the areas of student experience and campus culture since these had been identified early as important areas for discussion. As well, an environmental scan contained a thorough PESTLE analysis. These summaries were useful in creating awareness amongst stakeholders who may have been cognizant of the changes in their particular units or programmes, but not the overall impact across the institution since the launch of the Eyes High strategy in 2011.

The consultation process was formally launched in September 2017 under the banner of "Energizing Eyes High." The main consultation activities used for this process were similar to 2011, with the addition of an online survey as discussed in Chapter 3. There were also semi-structured external sessions with donors, alumni, and community leaders which were led by the president. Over 10,000 faculty, staff, students, and external stakeholders participated in the consultation activities, which was almost three times more than in 2011. About 35 focus groups where held with almost 900 participants and about 3,300 online surveys were completed. The remainder participated in the weekly polls, roving booths, or emails.

A key difference between the 2011 and 2016 consultation phases was the framing of the consultation activities. In 2011 the goal was to compare the University of Calgary to external peers to identify where larger programme changes were required to move the university forward. In 2016 the intent was to review internal practices and processes to identify the adjustments needed for the university to continue progress towards the Eyes High goals. Thus, there was minimal direct comparison to other universities. The tool used to shape the discussions was the ERRC grid, which was presented in Chapter 3. The ERRC grid was structured to identify specific factors influencing the success of teaching, research, and community engagement programmes, as well as student experience and campus culture.

The primary data were the factors identified and the explanations given for the recommended changes to them. Again, qualitative data techniques were used to analyse the information by creating categories and two layers of sub-categories for the identified themes. These findings were illustrated through word clouds (see Chapter 3), which reflected the factors (i.e., themes) identified and the number of times they were identified. Explanations, or the logic associated with an identified theme, were developed for the five most dominant words in the cloud via the comments provided from the focus group discussions and surveys. These word clouds were easily understood and focused attention on the factors that needed to be adjusted.

To communicate the feedback from the consultation process, presentations were made to each faculty as well as many departments, units, and student union committees. They consisted of a review of the engagement process, identification of the primary changes recommended via the word clouds, and the overall changes needed to ensure that the university continued towards its long term goals. In these feedback sessions, approximately 80% of faculty, staff, and students were comfortable with the approach and conclusions, and 20% disagreed, which would be expected on a diverse campus.

The analysed findings were then summarised in detailed reports for each pillar. The reports included descriptions of the consultation activities, methodologies used to analyse the data, demographic analyses of participants in relation to the university community, and the findings arising from the analysed data. The intent was to provide the campus with detailed feedback on what was heard.

Developing the Strategy

Once the consultation phase was complete, all the information gathered in the environmental scan and engagement process was integrated and analysed, as discussed in Chapter 4. New strategic opportunities were identified, with the most notable being the inclusion of "entrepreneurial thinking." The original strategy statement was revised to:

> The University of Calgary is a global intellectual hub located in Canada's most enterprising city. In this spirited, high-quality learning environment, students will thrive in programs made rich by research, hands-on experiences, and entrepreneurial thinking. By 2022, we will be recognized as one of Canada's top five research universities, fully engaging the communities we both serve and lead.
>
> (University of Calgary, 2017:p.3)

The addition of "entrepreneurial thinking" was an important component to reflect the changes occurring with the city of Calgary in terms of economic diversification, and the need to reflect a stronger entrepreneurial culture throughout the institution. There was significant debate with respect to the meaning of entrepreneurial thinking so it would be inclusive of all stakeholders and disciplines. The final definition included in the strategy was:

> Entrepreneurial thinking is being creative in finding innovative solutions. It involves taking initiative, exchanging knowledge across disciplines, being resourceful, and learning from experience. Entrepreneurial thinking is essential to enriching lives and advancing society.
>
> (University of Calgary, 2017:p.13)

The three foundational commitments in the 2011 strategy were retained with the addition of student experience and campus culture as cross-cutting priorities. Student experience and campus culture were defined in the strategy with input from stakeholders and the oversight committee. Each of the foundational commitments were further detailed through sections on "where we are," "where we're going," and "how we will get there" over the following five years. These were refreshed from the 2011 strategy.

After the strategy was finalised and approved, it was launched as part of the final celebration and legacy of the 50th anniversary in 2017. The name of the strategy—Eyes High—was retained because of its familiarity and endorsement on campus.

Executing the Strategy

Converting the revised Eyes High strategy to specific initiative development, operational decision-making, and resource allocation was done through refreshed academic and research plans. These refreshed plans were developed in parallel through a process co-led by the PVPA and VPR using the process described in Chapter 3. An important element throughout the process was ensuring that stakeholders were made aware of the impacts of the 2012–2017 academic and research plans, so the role and importance of these plans were communicated.

The resulting revised academic plan contained three priorities: (1) prioritising people, (2) connecting communities, and (3) driving innovation. For each of these priorities, the plan contains actions and timelines for completion. In total, there are 79 specific actions over the 2018–2023 time period (University of Calgary, 2018b). The research plan also contains three priorities, namely: (1) matching strengths with opportunities, (2) increasing research capacity, and (3) driving innovation. As in the case of the academic plan, there are actions for each priority, which total 23 for the research plan (University of Calgary, 2018c).

The "Matching Strengths with Opportunities" priority deserves further explanation due to the impact that this can have on an institution. In brief, this priority leads to the selection of strategic research themes where there is excellence, capacity, and opportunity. During the development of the research plan, there was an open process to solicit areas for consideration, which led to an evaluation and selection of six thematic areas. These areas received additional resources, recruitment of people (faculty and staff), and consideration in major research funding competitions and major philanthropic opportunities.

As part of executing the strategy, the 2011 KPIs were reviewed and modified. A total of 37 metrics resulted and formed the basis for further reporting along with qualitative impacts. The linkage of the strategy to the academic and research plans, to the business plan, and performance framework remained the same for the strategic plan period and in alignment with the steps in Chapter 5.

Future-Proofing

The use of KPIs and qualitative stories to highlight the impact of the energised Eyes High strategy continued, with 16 of 32 KPIs which had available peer comparator data being in the top five by 2018. Fluctuations in these KPIs relative to peers are expected from year to year, but they reveal an overall performance trend. One example of the impact of the strategy and plans is the growth in total research funding. From 2011 until 2018, there was a 48% growth in total research funding, which has placed the University of Calgary sixth nationally (University of Calgary, 2018a).

A broader measure of the impact of an institutional strategy can be taken from national and international rankings. There is an increasing trend in the global higher education sector to use these for competitive positioning of an institution, despite the drawbacks and limitations of these ranking systems. Since some global rankings place significant weight on reputational surveys (e.g., 33% to 50%), this can largely handicap younger universities which are building their international reputations. This has led to the development of sub-ranking categories such as "Top Universities Under 50 Years of Age" and "Top Golden Age Universities Founded After WWII" (QS, 2020). Overall, there has been consistent progress by the university with some recalibrations, when ranking systems change their methodology, for example. The University of Calgary has placed in the top 200 of global universities for some rankings, and for sub-ranking categories for younger institutions; it has placed highly in North America and globally, including being ranked number nine globally in the top 50 universities under 50. Although these ranking systems provide some value to institutional planning and measurement, "chasing rankings" as part of an institutional strategy can be distractive and should not be the focus of impact measurement.

The $1.3B CAD fundraising campaign continued to flourish with the new Eyes High strategy and, in particular, the focus on entrepreneurial thinking gained significant community support, including a $40M CAD donation to create the Hunter Hub for Entrepreneurial Thinking. The clear alignment of the institutional strategy and the campaign provided strong incentives for investment by community leaders and donors and, when completed, the campaign exceeded its initial goal of $1.3B CAD. Additionally, over the course of the Eyes High strategy from 2011, all three levels of government collectively invested over $900M CAD in strategic initiatives at the University of Calgary over and above regular operating or research programme funding.

The synergy between strategy and institutional culture as discussed in Chapter 6 was an important foundation for success. The employee engagement survey conducted every two years showed results that improved to the point where they benchmarked above private and public sector norms, meaning that the university was well above its peers in employee engagement and enablement. In particular, the survey results showed dramatic increases in areas of concern from the first survey, with the highest favourable response in 2017 of over 82% of faculty and staff stating that they understood the Eyes High strategy. Additionally, the largest increases from 2011 to 2017 in terms of favourable responses by faculty and staff were in the areas of the university being effectively managed and well run, and the university being among the top universities in Canada.

References

Adewale, A.R. & Esther, M.M. (2012) The relationship between stakeholders involvement in strategic planning and organisations performance a study of the university of Venda. *International Business & Economics Research Journal (IBER)*. 11 (11), 1175–1190. Available from: doi:10.19030/iber.v11i11.7366.

Aguinis, H. (2009) An expanded view of performance management. In: Smither, J.W. & London, M. (eds.) *Performance management: Putting research into action*. The professional practice series. San Francisco, Jossey-Bass, pp. 1–43.

Altbach, P.G., Reisberg, L. & Rumbley, L.E. (2009) *Trends in global higher education: Tracking an academic revolution*. Paris, United Nations Educational, Scientific and Cultural Organization.

Altmann, A. & Ebersberger, B. (2012) Universities in change: As a brief introduction. In: Altmann, A. & Ebersberger, B. (eds.) *Universities in change: Innovation, technology, and knowledge management*. New York, Springer, pp. 1–6.

Anderson, D., Johnson, R. & Milligan, B. (1999) *Strategic planning in Australian universities*. Department of Education, Training and Youth Affairs. Report number: 99/1.

Asheim, B.T. & Coenen, L. (2005) Knowledge bases and regional innovation systems: Comparing Nordic clusters. *Research Policy*. 34 (8), 1173–1190.

Baghai, M., Coley, S. & White, D. (2000) *The alchemy of growth*. London, Orion Books.

Balmer, J.M.T. & Greyser, S.A. (eds.) (2003) *Revealing the corporation: Perspectives on identity, image, reputation, corporate branding, and corporate-level marketing*. London, Routledge.

Barr, M.J. & McClellan, G.S. (2018) *Budgets and financial management in higher education*. Third edition. San Francisco, Jossey-Bass.

Berquist, W. (1992) *The four cultures of the academy*. San Francisco, Jossey Bass.

Blue Ocean Strategy. (2020) *ERRC grid*. Available from: www.blueoceanstrategy.com/tools/errc-grid/ [Accessed 15th February 2020].

Boost Labs. (2014) *Word clouds & the value of simple visualizations*. Available from: www.boostlabs.com/what-are-word-clouds-value-simple-visualizations/ [Accessed 27th March 2020].

Brew, A. (2003) Teaching and research: New relationships and their implications for inquiry-based teaching and learning in higher education. *Higher Education*

Research & Development. 22 (1), 3–18. Available from: doi:10.1080/07294360 32000056571.

Burgelman, R.A. (2002) Strategy as vector and the inertia of coevolutionary lock-in. *Administrative Science Quarterly.* 47 (2), 325–357.

Calgary Economic Development. (2020a) *Calgary: Census 2016.* Available from: https://calgaryeconomicdevelopment.com/assets/Uploads/Calgary-Census-2016-Infographic.pdf [Accessed 24th May 2020].

Calgary Economic Development. (2020b) *Economic indicators: Employment.* Available from: https://calgaryeconomicdevelopment.com/research-and-reports/ more-economic-indicators/employment/ [Accessed 24th May 2020].

Camera, L. (2019) *The higher education apocalypse.* Available from: www.usnews. com/news/education-news/articles/2019-03-22/college-closings-signal-start-of-a-crisis-in-higher-education/ [Accessed 23rd March 2020].

Chandler, N. (2013) Braced for turbulence: Understanding and managing resistance to change in the higher education sector. *Management.* 3 (5), 243–251. Available from: doi:10.5923/j.mm.20130305.01.

Checkoway, B. (2001) Renewing the civic mission of the American research university. *The Journal of Higher Education.* 72 (2), 125–147. Available from: doi:10.1 080/00221546.2001.11778875.

Chomos, S. (2017) *Employee engagement vs. culture surveys: What works best?* Available from: www.dynamicachievement.com/blog/2017/employee-engagement-vs-culture-surveys/ [Accessed 2nd June 2020].

Christensen, C.M. & Eyring, H.J. (2011) *The innovative university: Changing the DNA of higher education from the inside out.* San Francisco, Jossey-Bass.

Clark, B.R. (1998) *Creating entrepreneurial universities: Organizational pathways of transformation.* Bingley, UK, Emerald Group Publishing.

Clark, P., Chapleo, C. & Suomi, K. (2019) Branding higher education: An exploration of the role of internal branding on middle management in a university rebrand. *Tertiary Education and Management.* Available from: doi:10.1007/ s11233-019-09054-9.

Cohen, M.D. & March, J.G. (1974) *Leadership and ambiguity: The American college president.* New York, McGraw Hill.

Collins, J. (2001) *Good to great: Why some companies make the leap and others don't.* New York, Harper Collins.

Collis, D. & Rukstad, D.J. (2008) Can you say what your strategy is? *Harvard Business Review.* 86(4), 82–90.

Cornett, I. (2019) *Why effective communication requires repetition.* Available from: www.eaglesflight.com/blog/why-effective-communication-requires-repetition [Accessed 2nd June 2020].

Crow, M.M. & Dabars, W.B. (2015) *Designing the New American University.* Baltimore, Johns Hopkins University Press.

Daimler, M. (2018) *Why great employees leave "great cultures".* Available from: https://hbr.org/2018/05/why-great-employees-leave-great-cultures [Accessed 15th May 2020].

De Boer, H., Huisman, J., Klemperer, A., van der Meulen, B., Neave, G., Theisens, H. & van der Wende, M. (2002) *Academia in the 21st century: An analysis of trends and perspectives in higher education and research.* Adviesraad voor het Wetenschaps- en Technologie-beleid. Report number: AWT-Achtergrondstudie No. 28.

Dusst, E. & Winthrop, R. (2019) *Top 6 trends in higher education.* Available from: www.brookings.edu/blog/education-plus-development/2019/01/10/top-6-trends-in-higher-education/ [Accessed 5th March 2020].

Eckel, P. & Trower, C. (2019) Stop planning! *Inside Higher Ed.* Available from: www.insidehighered.com/views/2019/02/14/colleges-need-rethink-strategic-planning-opinion/ [Accessed 4th May 2020].

Education Dive Staff. (2020) *How many nonprofit colleges and universities have closed since 2016?* Available from: www.educationdive.com/news/tracker-college-and-university-closings-and-consolidation/539961/ [Accessed 23rd March 2020].

Etzkowitz, H. (2003) Research groups as 'quasi-firms': The invention of the entrepreneurial university. *Research Policy.* 32 (1), 109–121.

Etzkowitz, H. & Leydesdorff, L. (1999) The future location of research and technology transfer. *The Journal of Technology Transfer.* 24 (2–3), 111–123.

Etzkowitz, H., Webster, A., Gebhardt, C. & Terra, B.R.C. (2000) The future of the university and the university of the future: Evolution of ivory tower to entrepreneurial paradigm. *Research Policy.* 29 (2), 313–330. Available from: www.sciencedirect.com/science/article/pii/S0048733399000694/ [Accessed 23rd March 2020].

EY. (2018) *Can the universities of today lead learning for tomorrow? The university of the future.* Available from: https://assets.ey.com/content/dam/ey-sites/ey-com/en_au/topics/government-and-public-sector/ey-university-of-the-future-2030.pdf [Accessed 25th May 2020].

Garvin, D. & Roberto, M. (2001) What you don't know about making decisions. *Harvard Business Review.* 79 (8), 108–116.

Gavetti, G. (2012) PERSPECTIVE: Toward a behavioral theory of strategy. *Organization Science.* 23 (1), 267–285.

Gioia, D.A. & Chittipeddi, K. (1991) Sensemaking and sensegiving in strategic change initiation. *Strategic Management Journal.* 12 (6), 433–448. Available from: doi:10.1002/smj.4250120604.

Goldman, C.A. & Salem, H. (2015) *Getting the most out of university strategic planning: Essential guidance for success and obstacles to avoid.* RAND Corporation. Available from: www.rand.org/pubs/perspectives/PE157.html/ [Accessed 8th April 2020].

Goldstein, L.A. (2012) *Guide to college and university budgeting: Foundations for institutional effectiveness.* National Association of College and University Business Officers. ERIC number: ED595076. Available from: https://eric.ed.gov/?id=ED595076 [Accessed 8th April 2018].

Government of Alberta. (2017a) *Alberta research and innovation framework 2017.* Edmonton, Ministry of Economic Development and Trade, Government of Alberta.

Government of Alberta. (2017b) *2016 census of Canada: Visible minorities.* Available from: https://open.alberta.ca/dataset/4ccf4cb4-2768-4ae2-a656-48ecfbdbfd64/resource/eefd7eb9-3c05-4fc0-a100-865820655fd3/download/2016-census-visible-minorities.pdf [Accessed 24th May 2020].

Government of Canada. (2014) *Seizing Canada's moment: Moving forward in science, technology and innovation 2014.* Industry Canada, Government of Canada. Available from: www.ic.gc.ca/eic/site/113.nsf/vwapj/seizing_moment_ST-I_ summary-eng.pdf/$file/seizing_moment_ST-I_summary-eng.pdf [Accessed 24th May 2020].

Green, H. (2012) *Strategy ain't what it used to be.* Available from: www.forbes. com/sites/work-in-progress/2012/09/11/strategy-aint-what-it-used-to-be/#6 c9938dc6cd6/ [Accessed 8th April 2020].

Grey, C. (2001) Re-imagining relevance: A response to Starkey and Madan. *British Journal of Management.* 12, S27–S32.

Hattie, J. & Marsh, H.W. (1996) The relationship between research and teaching: A meta-analysis. *Review of Educational Research.* 66 (4), 507–542.

Heracleous, L. (2011) Introduction to the special issue on bridging the scholar—practitioner divide. *Journal of Applied Behavioral Science.* 47 (1), 5–7.

Heslin, P.A., Carson, J.B. & VandeWalle, D. (2009) Practical applications of goal-setting theory to performance management. In: Smither, J.W. & London, M. (eds.) *Performance management: Putting research into action.* The professional practice series. San Francisco, Jossey-Bass, pp. 89–114.

Hinton, K.E. (2012) *A practical guide to strategic planning in higher education.* Ann Arbor, Society for College and University Planning.

Hyter, M.C. (2020) *Measures for success.* Available from: www.kornferry.com/ insights/articles/measures-for-success [Accessed 2nd June 2020].

Indiana University School of Education. (2018) *The Carnegie classification of institutions of higher education.* Center for Postsecondary Research. Available from: https://carnegieclassifications.iu.edu/downloads/CCIHE2018-FactsFigures.pdf [Accessed 8th April 2020].

Institute of Corporate Directors. (2019) *Why culture is the board's job.* Available from: www.icd.ca/Resource-Centre/News-Publications/Director-Lens/Why-culture-is-the-board%E2%80%99s-job.aspx [Accessed 2nd June 2020].

Jones, G.A. (2014) An introduction to higher education in Canada. In: Joshi, K.M. & Paivandi, S. (eds.) *Higher education across nations volume 1.* Delhi, B.R. Publishing, pp. 1–38.

Kahneman, D., Lovallo, D. & Sibony, O. (2011) Before you make that big decision. *Harvard Business Review.* 89 (6), 50–60.

Kaplan, R.S. & Norton, D.P. (2005) The office of strategy management. *Harvard Business Review,* 83 (10), 72–80.

Kezar, A. & Eckel, P.D. (2002) The effect of institutional culture on change strategies in higher education: Universal principles or culturally responsive concepts? *The Journal of Higher Education.* 73 (4), 435–460. Available from: doi:10.1080/ 00221546.2002.11777159.

Kim, W.C. & Mauborgne, R. (2005) Blue ocean strategy: From theory to practice. *California Management Review.* 47 (3), 105–121.

Kim, W.C. & Mauborgne, R. (2014) *Blue ocean strategy, expanded edition: How to create uncontested market space and make the competition irrelevant.* Boston, Harvard Business Review Press.

Kinnerley, M. (2018) Indicators for measuring and managing performance. In: Strike, T. (ed.) *Higher education strategy and planning: A professional guide.* London, Taylor & Francis, pp. 213–227.

Kondrat, M.E. (1992) Reclaiming the practical: Formal and substantive rationality in social work practice. *Social Service Review.* 66 (2), 237–255.

Korman, J. (2019) *The benefits of framing culture as a management system.* Available from: https://sloanreview.mit.edu/article/the-benefits-of-framing-culture-as-a-management-system/?utm_source=newsletter&utm_medium=email&utm_content=Read%20the%20new%20article%20now%20%C2%BB&utm_campaign=Enews-GEN-10/10/19 [Accessed 2nd June 2020].

Kuh, G.D. & Whitt, E.J. (1988) *The invisible tapestry: Culture in American colleges and universities.* Association for the Study of Higher Education, Report number: 1.

Laredo, P. (2007) Revisiting the third mission of universities: Toward a renewed categorization of university activities? *Higher Education Policy.* 20 (4), 441–456.

Learned, E.P., Christensen, C.R., Andrews, K.R. & Guth, W.D. (1969) *Business policy: Text and cases.* New York, McGraw Hill.

Leih, S. & Teece, D. (2016) Campus leadership and the entrepreneurial university: A dynamic capabilities perspective. *Academy of Management Perspectives.* 30 (2), 182–210.

Liu, X. & White, S. (2001) Comparing innovation systems: A framework and application to China's transitional context. *Research Policy.* 30 (7), 1091–1114.

Mampaey, J. & Huisman, J. (2016) Branding of UK higher education institutions: An integrated perspective on the content and style of welcome addresses. *Recherches sociologiques et anthropologiques.* 47 (1), 133–148.

Martin, R.L. & Golsby-Smith, T. (2017) Management is much more than a science. *Harvard Business Review.* 95 (5), 128–135.

Mattie, J. (2007) *Meeting the challenges of enterprise risk management in higher education.* Washington, DC, National Association of College and University Business Officers (NJ1).

Mintzberg, H. (1994) The fall and rise of strategic planning. *Harvard Business Review.* 72 (1), 107–114.

Mintzberg, H. (1996) Musings on management. *Harvard Business Review.* 74 (4), 61–67.

Morphew, C.C., Fumasoli, T. & Stensaker, B. (2016) Changing missions? How the strategic plans of research-intensive universities in Northern Europe and North America balance competing identities. *Studies in Higher Education.* 43 (6), 1074–1078. Available from: doi:10.1080/03075079.2016.1214697.

Mowery, D.C. & Sampat, B.N. (2005) Universities in national innovation systems. In: Fagerberg, J., Mowery, D.C. & Nelson, R.R. (eds.) *The Oxford handbook on innovation.* New York, Oxford University Press, pp. 209–239.

Neave, G. (1989) Access to higher education : An overview. *Higher Education Policy.* 2 (1), 7–10. Available from: https://doi.org/10.1057/hep.1989.1.

Nelson, R.R. & Winter, S.G. (1982) The Schumpeterian tradeoff revisited. *The American Economic Review.* 72 (1), 114–132.

Nicolai, A.T. (2004) The bridge to the 'real world': Applied science or a 'schizophrenic tour de force'? *Journal of Management Studies.* 41 (6), 951–976.

NSC Research Center. (2019) *Spring 2019 term enrollment estimates*. Available from: https://nscresearchcenter.org/wp-content/uploads/CurrentTermEnrollmentReport-Spring-2019.pdf [Accessed 5th March 2020].

Ocasio, W. & Joseph, J. (2018) The attention-based view of great strategies. *Strategy Science*. 3 (1), 289–294.

Omerzel, D., Biloslavo, R. & Trnavcevic, A. (2011) Knowledge management and organisational culture in higher education institutions. *Journal for East European Management Studies*. 16 (2), 111–139.

Pai, F.Y., Yeh, T.M. & Huang, K.I. (2012) Professional commitment of information technology employees under depression environments. *International Journal of Electronic Business Management*. 10 (1), 17–28.

Parker, A. & Tritter, J. (2006) Focus group method and methodology: Current practice and recent debate. *International Journal of Research & Method in Education*. 29 (1), 23–37. Available from: doi:10.1080/01406720500537304.

Pavel, A.P. (2015) Global university rankings-a comparative analysis. *Procedia Economics and Finance*. 26, 54–63.

Pierce, S. (2017) Hope and denial are not strategies. *Inside Higher Ed*. Available from: www.insidehighered.com/views/2017/01/31/how-colleges-should-rethink-their-strategic-planning-processes-essay/ [Accessed 30th March 2020].

Porck, J.P., van Knippenberg, D., Tarakci, M., Ateş, N.Y., Groenen, P.J. & de Haas, M. (2018) Do group and organizational identification help or hurt intergroup strategic consensus? *Journal of Management*. 46 (2), 234–260. Available from: doi:10.1177/0149206318788434.

Porter, M.E. (1985) *Competitive strategy: Creating and sustaining superior performance*. New York, Free Press.

Porter, M.E. (1996) What is strategy? *Harvard Business Review*. 74 (6), 61–78.

Pritchard, J. (2018) Developing institutional strategy. In Strike, T. (ed.) *Higher education strategy and planning: A professional guide*. London, Taylor & Francis, pp. 49–68.

QS. (2020) *QS top 50 under 50 2020*. Available from: www.topuniversities.com/university-rankings-articles/top-50-under-50-next-50-under-50/qs-top-50-under-50-2020 [Accessed 15th May 2020].

Raynor, M. (2007) *The strategy paradox: Why committing to success leads to failure*. New York, Currency/Doubleday.

Robertson, S.L. & Olds, K. (2018) Locating universities in a globalising world. In: Strike, T. (ed.) *Higher education strategy and planning: A professional guide*. New York, Routledge, pp. 13–29.

Rumelt, R.P. (2012) *Good strategy/bad strategy: The difference and why it matters*. New York, Crown Publishers.

Schofer, E. & Meyer, J.W. (2005) The worldwide expansion of higher education in the twentieth century. *American Sociological Review*. 70 (6), 898–920.

SCUP. (2020) *Trends inside higher education*. Ann Arbor, The Society for College and University Planning, Spring.

Selzer, R. (2018) Smart, succinct and agile: Strategic planning in an age of uncertainty. *Inside Higher Ed*. Available from: www.insidehighered.com/content/

smart-succinct-and-agile-strategic-planning-age-uncertainty/ [Accessed 8th April 2020].

Shin, L.D. (2017) *Strategic thinking and planning in higher education: A focus on the future*. Washington, DC, AGB Press.

Simon, H.A. (1976) From substantive to procedural rationality. In: Kastelein, T.J., Kuipers, S.K., Nijenhuis, W.A. & Wagenaar, G.R. (eds.) *25 years of economic theory*. Boston, Springer, pp. 65–86.

Slaughter, S. & Leslie, L.L. (1997) *Academic capitalism: Politics, policies, and the entrepreneurial university*. Baltimore, Johns Hopkins University Press.

Smith, P. (2020) A GPS for learning and work. *Inside Higher Ed*. Available from: www.insidehighered.com/digital-learning/blogs/rethinking-higher-education/gps-learning-and-work/ [Accessed 6th April 2020].

Smither, J.W. & London, M. (eds.) (2009) *Performance management: Putting research into action*. The professional practice series. San Francisco, Jossey-Bass.

Statistics Canada. (2020) *Annual demographic estimates*. Available from: www150.statcan.gc.ca/n1/pub/71-607-x/71-607-x2020003-eng.htm [Accessed 24th May 2020].

Stensaker, B. (2007) The relationship between branding and organisational change. *Higher Education Management and Policy*. 19 (1), 1–17. Available from: doi:10.1787/hemp-v19-art1-en.

Strike, T. (2018) Introduction. In: Strike, T. (ed.) *Higher education strategy and planning: A professional guide*. New York, Routledge, pp. 1–10.

Strike, T., Hanlon, M. & Foster, D. (2018) The functions of strategic planning. In: Strike, T. (ed.) *Higher education strategy and planning: A professional guide*. New York, Routledge, pp. 30–48.

Sull, D., Homkes, R. & Sull, C. (2015) Why strategy execution unravels—and what to do about it. *Harvard Business Review*. 93 (3), 57–66.

Sull, D., Turconi, S., Sull, C. & Yoder, J. (2017) How to develop strategy for execution. *MIT Sloan Management Review*. Special Issue, 1–6. Available from: https://sloanreview.mit.edu/article/how-to-develop-strategy-for-execution/ [Accessed 4th May 2020].

Tagg, J. (2012) Why does the faculty resist change? *Change: The Magazine of Higher Learning*. 44 (1), 6–15. Available from: doi:10.1080/00091383.2012.635987.

Tamburri, R. (2013) *University rankings gain influence, despite obvious drawbacks*. Available from: www.universityaffairs.ca/news/news-article/university-rankings-gain-influence-despite-obvious-drawbacks/ [Accessed 24th March 2020].

Taye, M., Sang, G. & Muthanna, A. (2019) Organizational culture and its influence on the performance of higher education institutions: The case of a state university in Beijing. *International Journal of Research*. 8 (2), 77–90. Available from: doi:10.5861/ijrse.2019.3026.

Teasdale, S. (2002) Culture eats strategy for breakfast! *Journal of Innovation in Health Informatics*. 10 (4), 195–196.

Thompson, C.S. (2017) Involvement in and attitudes towards strategic planning in their institutions. *Educational Planning*. 24 (1), 7–21.

Tierney, W. (1988) Organizational culture in higher education: Defining the essentials. *The Journal of Higher Education.* 59 (1), 2–21. Available from: doi:10.108 0/00221546.1988.11778301.

Tierney, W. (1991) Organizational culture in higher education: Defining the essentials. In: Peterson, M. (ed.) *ASHE reader on organization and governance.* Needham Heights, Ginn Press, pp. 126–139.

Tierney, W.G. & Lanford, M. (2018) Institutional culture in higher education. In: Teixeira, P. & Shin, J. (eds.) *Encyclopedia of international higher education systems and institutions.* Dordrecht, Springer, pp. 1–9. Available from: doi:10.1007/978-94-017-9553-1.

Tranfield, D. & Starkey, K. (1998) The nature, social organization and promotion of management research: Towards policy. *British Journal of Management.* 9 (4), 341–353.

Trivellas, P. & Dargenidou, D. (2009) Organisational culture, job satisfaction and higher education service quality: The case of Technological Educational Institute of Larissa. *The TQM Journal.* 21 (4), 382–399. Available from: doi:10.1108/17542730910965083.

U15. (2020) *U15 group of Canadian research universities—about us.* Available from: http://u15.ca/about-us [Accessed 24th May 2020].

UNESCO Institute for Statistics. (2014) *Higher education in Asia, expanding out, expanding up: The rise of graduate education and university research.* UNSESCO. Available from: doi:10.15220/978-92-9189-147-4-en.

Universities Canada. (2020) *Member universities.* Available from: www.univcan.ca/universities/member-universities/ [Accessed 24th May 2020].

University of Calgary. (2011) *Eyes high strategy 2011–2016.* Available from: https://ucalgary.ca/research/files/research/eyes_high-2011-vision-and-strategy.pdf [Accessed 4th May 2020].

University of Calgary. (2016) *Eyes high consultation.* Available from: www.ucalgary.ca/eyeshigh/consultation [Accessed 14th April 2020].

University of Calgary. (2017) *Eyes high strategy 2017–2022.* Available from: www.ucalgary.ca/live-uc-ucalgary-site/sites/default/files/teams/17/17-UNV-016-Eyes%20High%20strategy%20document-digital-FINAL.pdf [Accessed 4th May 2020].

University of Calgary. (2018a) *Community report.* Available from: https://go.ucalgary.ca/rs/161-OLN-990/images/CommunityReport2018.pdf [Accessed 24th May 2020].

University of Calgary. (2018b) *Academic plan 2018–2023.* Available from: https://ucalgary.ca/provost/sites/default/files/teams/1/academic_plan_20180130_web.pdf [Accessed 24th May 2020].

University of Calgary. (2018c) *Research plan 2018–2023.* Available from: https://ucalgary.ca/research/files/research/research_plan_20180205_web.pdf [Accessed 24th May 2020].

Usher, A. (2018a) *Academic service (third mission).* Higher Education Strategy Associates. Available from: http://higheredstrategy.com/academic-service/ [Accessed 23rd March 2020].

Usher, A. (2018b) *2003–04: The historical hinge of international rankings*. Higher Education Strategy Associates. Available from: http://higheredstrategy.com/2003-04-the-historical-hinge-of-international-rankings/ [Accessed 23rd March 2020].

Usher, A. (2018c) *League-table rankings, sumo style*. Higher Education Strategy Associates. Available from: http://higheredstrategy.com/league-table-rankings-sumo-style/ [Accessed 23rd March 2020].

Usher, A. (2019a) *Strategic planning for ambiguous organizations*. Higher Education Strategy Associates. Available from: http://higheredstrategy.com/strategic-planning-for-ambiguous-organizations/ [Accessed 23rd March 2020].

Usher, A. (2019b) *Performance-based funding 101: Alternatives and next steps*. Higher Education Associates. Available from: http://higheredstrategy.com/performance-based-funding-101-the-indicators/ [Accessed 8th April 2018].

Van de Ven, A.H. & Johnson, P.E. (2006) Knowledge for theory and practice. *Academy of Management Review*. 31 (4), 802–821.

Vermeulen, F. (2017) *Breaking bad habits: Defy industry norms and reinvigorate your business*. Boston, Harvard Business Review Press.

Wang, J.X. (2010) *Lean manufacturing: Business bottom-line based*. Boca Raton, CRC Press.

Webb, A. (2020) The 11 sources of disruption every company must monitor. *MIT Sloan Management Review*. Spring issue. Available from: https://sloanreview.mit.edu/article/the-11-sources-of-disruption-every-company-must-monitor/ [Accessed 30th March 2020].

Webster, D.S. (1985) Does research productivity enhance teaching? *Educational Record*. 66 (4), 60–62.

Weingarten, H.P., Hicks, M., Jonker, L., Smith, C. & Arnold, H. (2015) *Canadian postsecondary performance: IMPACT 2015*. Higher Education Quality Council of Ontario. Available from: www.heqco.ca/SiteCollectionDocuments/HEQCO_Canadian_Postsecondary_Performance_Impact2015.pdf [Accessed 8th April 2020].

Welbourne, T.M. (2016) The potential of pulse surveys: Transforming surveys into leadership tools. *Employment Relations Today*. 43 (1), 33–39. Available from: doi:10.1002/ert.21548.

Yorke, M. (2004) Institutional research and its relevance to the performance of higher education institutions. *Journal of Higher Education Policy and Management*. 26 (2), 141–152.

Youtie, J. & Shapira, P. (2008) Building an innovation hub: A case study of the transformation of university roles in regional technological and economic development. *Research Policy*. 37 (8), 1188–1204.

Zakaria, F. (2015) *In defense of a liberal education*. New York, WW Norton & Company.

Index

students); support 62, **64–65**, 72, 74,
78, 88, 92, 95
Starkey, K. 3
Statistics Canada 102
STEEP 36
Stensaker, B. 4, 63
strategic change 19, **22**–23; incremental
22, **28**; transformational change 14,
84, 86, 95
strategic opportunities *see* opportunities
strategic planning: activities 14,
39–**40**; campus leaders 20 (*see
also* engagement; ERRC grid);
expectations 21, 28, 32; governance
15, 25, **28**; launch 40, 64–65;
operational structure 25–26; phases
13–**14**; principles **13**; purpose 19 (*see
also* strategy canvas); support 21
strategic thinking 70, **71**
strategy: assessment 68, 74–75, 77,
80, **83**–84, 90–91, **100** (*see also*
blue ocean); bridge 5, 51, **71**;
challenges 79, 94; contract with
president xv, 12, **16**; creating *52*–54
(*see also* culture; decision making);
disruptions 78; document 61, 63,
64, **66**; effectiveness 5, 39, 52, 65,
67, 75–76 (*see also* engagement);
execution 15, 38, 62, 67–74, 80–**83**,
86; faculty plans 20; failures 9–11,
15, **16**, 67, 71, 78, 88; feasibility
57; function 5–6; future orientation
16; goals 8, 11, 51, 61; identity
64; internal dynamics 2 (*see also*
line-of-sight; narrative; operational
plan); outcomes xiii–iv, 1–2, 7–9, 11,
16, 51, **65**, 71, 79, 95; plan 61, **64**;
renewal 19, 80 (*see also* president;
red ocean); report 61; research xii,
5; simplicity 6; statement 51–52, 61,
65; sub-strategies 93; success 11, 13
strategy canvas 41–*43*, 46–47, **50**
Strike, T. 5
students xii, 1, 3–4, 8, 10–12, 18–19,
21, 24, 30, **34**–35, 38, 41, *48*–49,
57–*58*, 63, 77–79, 89, 92, **100**
Sull, C. 10, 53
Sull, D. 10, 53
Suomi, K. 63

survey 91; assess progress 89; benefits
39, 46, 89; data 47, 54; donors
90; employee engagement 81,
96–99, **100**; ERRC grid 47; exit 96;
government leaders 90; limitations
46, **50**; on-line 39, 46; ranking 4;
reputation 89–90; results 33, 54,
72–*73*, 90–**91**; stakeholders **91**;
structure 47, **50**
SWOT analysis **53**–**55**, 60, **65**

Tagg, J. 20
Tamburri, R. 4
Tarakci, M. 1, 9
Taye, M. 9, 84
teaching *see* pillars
Teasdale, S. 8
Teece, D. 2, 8
tension: internal 2; pillars 2–3, 15
Terra, B.R.C. 4
Theisens, H. 3
Thompson, C.S. 32
Tierney, W. 9, 20, 84, 85, 86, 92, 93,
94, 95, 96
time horizons 6–8, 78
Tranfield, D. 3
trends: academic 30; assessing impact
14, 16, 30, 35; best practices
35; conflicting 47, **50**; declining
enrollments 1; disruptive i, 10, 78;
identifying **34**; knowledge of 21,
30; massification 1; operational 72;
pillars 35; presentation of 36, 47–48;
response to 6, 8, 11, 21, 41; scans
35; sensemaking 53; socio-cultural
35, 54; strategic implications **56**;
strategy alignment 17, 19, 67; in
survey data 47; technology 35
triple helix 4
Tritter, J. 39
Trivellas, P. 85
Trnavcevic, A. 85
Trower, C. 57, 68
trust 98
Turconi, S. 10, 53

U15 76, 102
UNESCO Institute for Statistics 1
Universities Canada 102

Printed in the United States
by Baker & Taylor Publisher Services